37 ¾ Miles . . .
and So Much More

The Isle of Man T.T. Races

Mike Hennecks

Graham Beasant

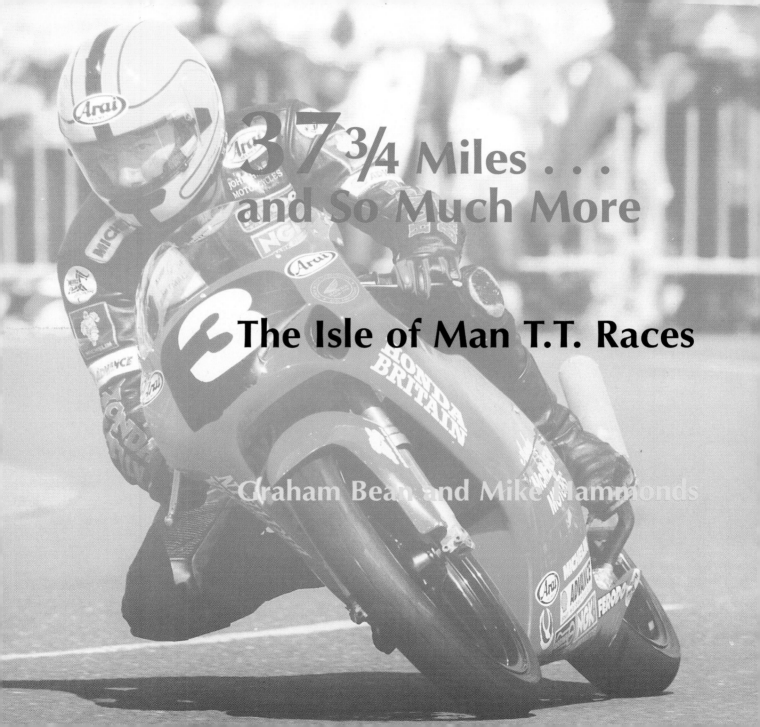

37 3/4 Miles . . . and So Much More

The Isle of Man T.T. Races

Graham Bean and Mike Hammonds

Published 1999 by

The Manx Experience
45 Slieau Dhoo : Tromode Park : Douglas : Isle of Man : IM2 5LG : British Isles

ISBN No 1 873120 41 9

Originated by
The Manx Experience

Printed by
Mannin Media Group Limited
Spring Valley Industrial Estate : Braddan : Isle of Man : IM2 2QS : British Isles

FOREWORD

by Charlie Williams

Courtesy Mike Hammonds

Graham Bean and Mike Hammonds are typical of many T.T. enthusiasts, but they take their enthusiasm further than most. Not only have they worked tirelessly in the interest of the T.T. Supporters Club, but now they find time to write *37¾ Miles and So Much More.*

An event that will be 100 years old in 2007 has got to be very special whatever it is, and the T.T. is no exception - justifiably having many books written about it.

This book is an amalgam of previously recorded facts and many interesting "snippets", probably only known to a few of the T.T's most ardent buffs.

The thrills of racing on the Mountain Course covered in this book have been enhanced by superb action photographs - many of which have not been seen until now.

I was particularly interested to read the chapters covering the T.T. careers of both Robert Dunlop and the late Klaus Klein, two riders for whom I have the greatest respect.

Klaus took his racing very seriously but away from the track was a real party animal; we had a lot of fun at the T.T. Carnival held in the now defunct Palace Lido where Klaus was generally star of the show.

If there is, or has been a more tenacious or determined rider than Robert Dunlop, then I have yet to meet him. The injuries from his crash at Ballaugh in 1994 were horrendous, yet he overcame his permanent disabilities to win the 125cc Race of 1998, having shattered the lap record in practice.

37¾ Miles and So Much More gets under the surface of the T.T.

A very interesting read . . .

The T.T. Mountain Course

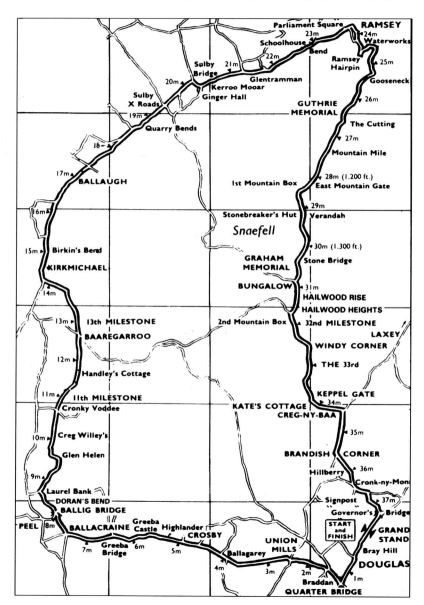

CONTENTS

The St John's Course

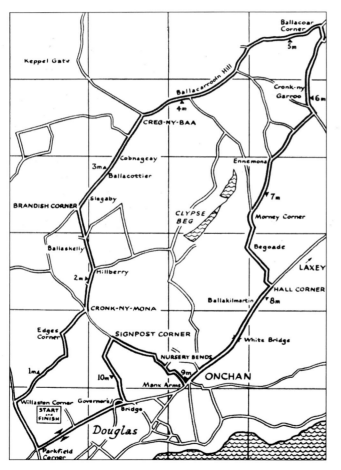

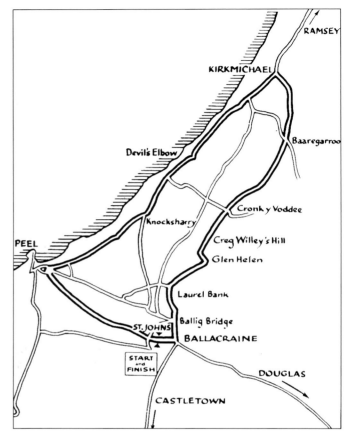

The Clypse
Course

INTRODUCTION

After a lifetime of watching the T.T. races, following the trials, tribulations and successes of those involved and working for many years on the T.T. Supporters Club twice yearly magazine, we thought the time was right for us to publish our first book.

Rather than follow one particular theme, we've decided to cover a variety of facets - the triumph over adversity of Robert Dunlop, the golden years of Honda, the determination and skill of top foreign competitor, Klaus Klein, the teamwork of the Kiwis in winning the Maudes Trophy, the increased participation of lady riders in the solo classes and the rise and fall of 50cc racing on the Mountain Course. We've also included many shorter articles and many factual items; running throughout is our A-Z of the T.T. and an analysis of increasing lap speeds. As the title of the book suggests . . . *37 3/4 Miles and So Much More.*

Naturally, we could not have managed such an undertaking on our own - our thanks go to Les Eanor for his patience and technical input; to nine times T.T. winner, Charlie Williams for agreeing to write the Foreword, and to photographers John Burness, Nick Nicholls, Peter Wilcock, Eric Whitehead, Albert Cooper of The Mirror and the FoTTofinders Archive Research System whose expertise has added drama to the text.

Graham Bean and Mike Hammonds

Mike Hailwood at the exit from Governor's Bridge
Courtesy Island Photographics

IN THE BEGINNING

In compiling this book we thought it appropriate to take a careful look at the years prior to the Great War to establish just how the T.T. Races evolved into the world's greatest annual festival of motorcycling.

It was the Marquis de Mouzilly St. Mars who was instrumental in developing an event for motorcycles similar to that of the Car T.T. - hence the St. Mars Trophy, which featured a figure of Mercury, the God of Speed, on a Winged Wheel, was awarded to the winner of the 'singles' class. Competitors in the 'twin' cylinder class competed for a trophy presented by Dr. Hele-Shaw. There were also cash awards, £25 for the winners, £15 (runners up) and £10 (third place).

The triangular St. Johns Course (15 miles 1,430 yards in length) was deemed to be more appropriate for motorcycles than the Mountain Course used by the racing cars of the day and so twenty-five of the twenty-six entrants lined up alongside the Village Green at St. Johns on a bitterly cold morning in late May 1907. There was no limit to engine capacity, but single cylinder

machines were required to cover at least 90 miles and twins 75 miles on a gallon of petrol. The petrol, supplied by the ACU, had a specific gravity of 0.175 to 0.725 at 60°F and was issued in two portions - at the start and the balance after five of the ten laps, when riders were called in for a ten minute halt.

The start was made a few minutes after 10 am on the 28th May with competitors going off in pairs at two minute intervals. The race card of the day read:

Single Cylinder Class

1.	3½ hp Triumph	F. Hulbert
2.	3½ hp Triumph	J. Marshall
3.	Matchless-JAP 3½ hp	H. A. Collier
4.	Matchless-JAP 3½ hp	C. R. Collier
5.	3½ hp Brown	R. M. Brice
6.	4 hp Roc	F. Winter
8.	3 hp Rex	J. C. Smyth
9.	3½ hp Rex	W. A. Jacobs
10.	3½ hp Rex	F. W. Applebee
11.	3½ hp Ayton-Riley Special	R. W. Ayton
12.	3 hp NSU	J. D. Hamilton
14.	3 hp NSU	M.Geiger (Germany)
15.	3½ hp Thomas Silver	T. Silver
16.	3½ hp Triumph	S. Webb

17.	3 hp G-D	J. P. Le Grand
18.	3½ hp Triumph	R. W. Duke
19.	Royal Cavendish - 4 hp JAP	G. Horner

Twin Cylinder Class

20.	5 hp Rex	O. C. Godfrey
21.	Vindec Special 6 hp Peugeot	
		W. H. Wells (USA)
22.	Norton 5 hp Peugeot	H. R. Fowler
23.	5 hp Kerry	H. Martin
24.	BAT - 6 hp JAP	T. H. Tessier
25.	Vindec Special 6 hp Peugeot	J. A. Dent
26.	6 hp Rex	W. M. Heaton
27.	5 hp Rex	F. Applebee Jnr

And so Hulbert and Marshall pushed away to start one of the great spectacles in the sporting world.

42.91 mph – 1907
Twin Cylinder Class
Rem Fowler (Norton)
Fastest Lap
first T.T. meeting

Marshall's Triumph machine was the first to return, closely followed by Charlie Collier who soon took the lead, never to be headed again. He won the Single Cylinder Class covering the 158 miles in 4 hours 8 mins 8 secs at an average speed of 38.22 mph. The honour of making the fastest lap went to his brother, Harry, at 41.81 mph in finishing third, Marshall having secured the runner-up slot.

Rem Fowler (No.22) finished fourth on the roads to win the Twin Cylinder Class at an average speed of 36.22 mph with a fastest lap of 42.91 mph.

The doubtful honour of being the first rider to crash in a T.T. race went to W. A. Jacobs on his Rex who had a "smash", as the *I.O.M Times and General Advertiser* put it, "on the first run". The newspaper also reported several early incidents - "Applebee, Jnr, punctured on the first circuit, but continued; Wells stopped at the end of the second lap to tighten his driving belt; Horner stopped, saying that he could not possibly complete the course with his allowance of fuel, but was prepared to try to half time, and Charlie Collier had a cup of hot Oxo while his machine was being refuelled!" The most dramatic incident occurred in front of the Timekeeper's stand when Oliver Godfrey's machine was suddenly enveloped in flames. Apparently there was a fuel leak where the supply pipe entered the tank; a drop had fallen on the red hot cylinder and the vapour was ignited by a spark from the magneto.

At the end of the race Charlie Collier finished with 30 ounces of petrol in the tank and one in the carburettor. Competitors had to finish with 20 ounces to spare, so Collier was 11 ounces to the good. As *The Times* stated: "This may be regarded as cheap travelling - about two shillings worth of petrol for 150 odd miles!"

The T.T. Races of 1907 were a

A

Reg Armstrong

This well-educated Dubliner's T.T. career only lasted six years, but it was certainly eventful. Second string to Geoff Duke at both Norton and Gilera, he will be best remembered for his dramatic victory in the 1952 Senior. After Duke retired at the end of lap 4 with clutch trouble an epic battle ensued between Armstrong (Norton) and Les Graham (MV Agusta). After overhauling Graham the Irishman went on to win only for his chain to snap and drag along the ground as he crossed the finish line. Friday the 13th proved to be a lucky day for Reg Armstrong!

Many a tale to tell ... Reg Armstrong flanked by John Hartle (left) and Bob McIntyre on the starting grid for the 1961 Senior.
Courtesy FoTTofinders Archive Research System

B

Bianchi.

MV Agusta, Moto Guzzi, Ducati and Mondial have all provided victories for Italian engineering on the Mountain Course, but some marques, notably the Milan based Bianchi firm, have been less successful, despite employing some top line riders of their day. The company first tackled the course in 1926, securing three finishes, but then laid dormant in T.T. terms until 1960 when it returned with a vengeance, entering seven vertical lightweight twins. It was really part of a massive publicity exercise which, unfortunately, went embarrassingly wrong as only two machines, in the hands of

Osvaldo Perfetti lines up his Bianchi twin for Governor's Bridge.
Courtesy FoTTofinders Archive Research System

Derek Minter and development rider, Osvaldo Perfetti, made the starting grid. Minter's machine expired on the first lap; the Italian, in his only T.T. race, gamely came home ninth. The services of Scotsmen Bob McIntyre and Alistair King were secured for the '61 Junior. Both retired with gearbox problems aboard their vertical twins, which weighed nearly 300lbs and, as it was claimed, produced 48hp at 10,500rpm. Everyone respected the Bianchi's incredible speed - but it rarely kept going.

decided success although, surprisingly, twelve of the entrants never raced at the event again. Both overseas competitors, Geiger from Germany and American Wells, however, did return; two of the original entrants H. Martin and F. W. Applebee continued racing on the Island until the early 1920s. The original field contained five future winners, Collier again in 1910, his brother Harry who won the Singles in 1909 and Marshall (1908 - Singles), Applebee Junior (Senior - 1912) and Godfrey who won the first Senior held on the Mountain Course. Rem Fowler rode in five more races but only managed a highest place of 16th.

And so T.T. Racing had begun - many innovations took place between 1907 and the onset of the Great War:

53.15 mph – 1910
Twin Cylinder Class
H. H. Bowden (B.A.T.)
Fastest Lap
St. John's Circuit

Pedals were banned for the 1908 meeting and the petrol allowance was changed to 100 and 80 miles for singles and twins respectively. The T.T. of 1909 provided the first occasion on which the event became a race pure and simple, for in that year the limit of speed by petrol consumption was abandoned.

How were the competitors informed of their position in the early races? No pit signals - instead colleagues ran alongside and passed on the relevant information as they pushed or pedalled up Creg Willys.

St. Johns School provided a blackboard for the results service!

Another tradition was started in 1908. The first 'Race Marshals' were signed in as Special Constables for the duration of the meeting by the Governor of the Island.

The Governor was involved in the initiation of another event in 1909 that was to prove to be traditional - the first public prize-giving, held at the Palace Ballroom, which used to stand on the site just behind where we now find the Stakis Hotel.

A new aroma arrived in 1910 - Castrol R!

For 1911, two very important changes were made - obviously the course was changed to include the climb over Snaefell Mountain, but for the first time there was a Junior T.T. Race - singles being limited to 300cc and twins to 340cc The Senior Race was divided into singles (500cc) and twins (585cc).

Two events of note during the races of 1911 - the first tragedy and the first exclusion. Victor Surridge was killed during practice at Glen

C

Clypse Course.

From 1954 to 1959 both Lightweight and Sidecar races were run over the 10.79 mile long Clypse Course. The machines started on Glencrutchery Road, turned right at Parkfield Corner (St. Ninian's traffic lights), right again at Willaston Corner and joined the T.T. course at Cronk-ny-Mona travelling in the reverse direction up to Creg-ny-Baa. A sharp right was taken here and a narrow twisty section negotiated before another right at Ballacoar above Laxey. The course joined the coast road at the top of the Whitebridge Hill - a steep descent into Onchan, right at the Manx Arms, left at Signpost Corner, down to Governor's Bridge, avoiding the dip, and back on to the Start and Finish straight. It was named after the area it surrounded.

1957 Sidecar T.T. on the Clypse Course; Jack Beeton with Charlie Billingham.

D

Freddy Dixon.

Freddy Dixon lays claim to be the only man to win T.T.s on two, three and four wheels. He won the first Sidecar Race (1923) on his Douglas, the 1927 Junior on a HRD and the 1933 Mannin Beg Round - Douglas Car Race in a Riley. It was his three wheeled victory that is the most noteworthy . . . his outfit could bank over for cornering! A strong passenger was required to operate the two long levers either side of the sidecar which enabled the combination to "lean". . . Walter Denny proved to be ideal, with the pair winning the three lap race in 2 hours 7 mins 48 secs at an average speed of 53.15mph.

Dixon and Denny with their Douglas outfit equipped with levers and number plate?

Courtesy FoTTofinders Archive Research System

Helen and Charlie Collier was disqualified from second place in the Senior for taking on fuel while stopped on the course.

A one-off in 1913, when each race occupied two days; the idea being to make it more difficult as it was not permissible to make any adjustments to the machines between the finish on the first day and the commencement on the second day. The Juniors, who wore blue waistcoats, did two laps on the first day, and Seniors, red waistcoats, three. The survivors, or 75% of the starters, whichever was the smaller,

among both classes raced for four laps on the second day - in a massed start! Prior to 1913 only a basic scorecard kept spectators informed, but now an official programme gave greater insight.

Another tradition began in 1914 as a result of a fatal accident involving T. Bateman at Keppel Gate - compulsory use of safety helmets.

Up to 1914 the start area had been on Quarter Bridge Road, it was now changed to the top of Bray Hill on the outside of the course with a designated pit area. The Course, at this time, did not include Signpost

Corner, Bedstead, The Nook, Governor's Bridge or Glencrutchery Road; all that changed in 1920, but that's another story.

**50.11 mph – 1911
Senior
Frank Phillip (Scott)
Fastest Lap first year
Mountain Course**

ROBERT DUNLOP
Triumph Over Adversity

Few, if any, who witnessed the Newcomer's Race at the Diamond Jubilee of the Manx Grand Prix in 1983 would have realised its significance. Winner of the race was twenty-two year old Robert Dunlop who beat twenty-one year old Steve Hislop by 62.6 seconds and third was nineteen year old Ian Lougher a further 34.4 seconds behind. Never in the history of the Manx Grand Prix have the first three in a race gone on to have such illustrious careers in the T.T. Dunlop, Hislop and Lougher have amassed at least seventeen victories between them with Lougher being the first rider to hold both the 125cc and the 250cc lap records since Bill Ivy.

Robert announced after the race that he would contest the T.T. in 1984, Hislop and Lougher decided to give the Manx another year, although Lougher entered and came runner up in the 1984 Historic T.T. Dunlop's decision had been swayed by his winning time which would have given him sixteenth position and a bronze replica in the 350cc T.T. of that year.

Elder brother Joey first encouraged Robert to go racing, it

was an attempt to stop him from tearing around the local roads and falling off !! Joey gave him his first bike, a 250cc Seeley, and also lent him a set of his leathers. The first race was a non event with the bike failing to fire up at the start, never-the-less the bug had bitten and from then the racing would be confined to the race track and not the public highway. His love for the roads, however, was transferred to his racing where he excelled and he

Robert Dunlop powers away from the start on his way to winning the 1991 125cc T.T.
Courtesy John Burness

had the ambition of emulating brother Joey by winning a T.T. Race on the Isle of Man.

Robert entered his 347cc Yamaha in the Senior and Premier Classic T.T's. in 1984. A steady practice week saw him qualify 34th fastest in the Senior with a lap of 104.26 mph. and 18th fastest in the Classic with a lap of 104.92 mph. both set on Thursday afternoon. He also found time to help older brother Joey by doing a couple of laps on his 250cc machine to run it in. The Senior Race, which was won by Rob McElnea, will probably be best remembered for the controversial way in which race leader Joey

Dunlop failed to finish, stopping just ten miles from the chequered flag. There was a lot of conjecture as to whether Joey had run out of petrol or not; the official reason given was that his Honda had a broken crankshaft. Dunlop Junior did finish the race and came a very creditable fourteenth with a race average of 106.75 mph gaining a bronze replica. The Classic Race saw

Robert gain a silver replica with a race average of 106.83 mph when he finished twelfth and thus concluded a steady and successful baptism to T.T. racing. One could not have blamed Robert if he had thought that competing on the Mountain Course was not as hard as he had been led to believe. If this thought ever did cross his mind, the coming years would show him what an unforgiving place it can be.

Shipwrecked

Joey Dunlop's traditional way of transporting his bikes and himself to the Isle of Man was by fishing boat from a small port in Strangford Lough, Northern Ireland. For the 1985 T.T. Joey teamed up with brother Robert and fellow riders Brian Reid, Sam McClements and Noel Hudson to take their bikes across to the Island. In the early hours of Sunday morning the 26th of May the fishing boat *Tornamona* set sail for the Isle of Man with thirteen people on board, including the Dunlop brothers and Noel Hudson. At 0015 hours Belfast coastguards received an emergency May Day

---

E

Riders from Eire.

Probably the most famous was Stanley Woods, the Toffee Maker from Dublin, who dominated the T.T. scene in his day with ten victories on four different makes of machine - Cotton, Norton, Guzzi and Velocette - between 1923 and 1939. The most recent success story to come out of the Republic belongs to Eddie Laycock who took his EMC to victory in the 1987 Junior Race at an average of 108.52mph. He followed this up by winning the first 400cc Supersport Race two years later.

Eddie Laycock negotiating Quarter Bridge with utmost care during the 1990 T.T. *Courtesy FoTTofinders Archive Research System*

**54.69 mph – 1923
Harry Langdon
(Scott)
Fastest Lap
First sidecar T.T.**

call and launched the Portaferry Lifeboat to go to the aid of a fishing boat just off Strangford Lough. Aboard the *Tornamona* the riders had just bedded down to go to sleep when there was a crash as the boat hit the rocks and quickly started to take in water. All on board took to the life rafts, except the Captain who stayed with his ship. Due to the rough sea conditions Donaghadee Lifeboat was also launched as was the rescue helicopter from 72 Squadron of the Royal Airforce. The lifeboats towed the life rafts to safety and as this happened the *Tornamona* sank in thirty feet of water along with eight bikes worth over £60,000, the Captain having been rescued.

The riders, none the worse for their experience, assisted in rescuing the bikes from the Loch when daylight broke. Fortunately for Joey, his Honda Britain bikes were transported separately to the Island, however, Robert's 250 and 350cc bikes went down along with Sam McClements's FZ750 Yamaha, Brian Reid's 500 and 750cc machines and Noel Hudson's 250, 350 and 500cc bikes. Removing the bikes from the sea was the easy part, for they then had to be completely stripped and cleaned to remove all traces of the salt water and then transported to the Island. It was all a far cry from less than twenty four hours before when Robert Dunlop had won the 250cc race at Cookstown and taken the lead in the Ulster Championship.

Robert eventually arrived on the Isle of Man in time to practice on

Wednesday having had problems cleaning his 247cc E.M.C. Rotax which had started to corrode with the effects of the sea water. He qualified in seventeenth place with a lap of 103.78 mph on Friday evening on the Rotax for the Junior Race, a lowly twenty-fourth for the 250cc Production T.T. at 86.67 mph and finally in thirty-seventh place at 104.55 mph on his 350cc Yamaha for the Senior T.T. Race week brought mixed fortunes for the young Dunlop, with a retirement at Parliament Square on the third lap of

(Top)
Robert exiting Ramsey during his ill-fated 1986 Formula 2 Race.
Courtesy Eric Whitehead

The J.P.S. Norton at Braddan Bridge on the first lap of the 1990 Formula One Race
Courtesy Eric Whitehead

the Junior Race, achieving a very creditable sixth place in the 250cc Production Race to win a bronze replica and finally being the eighth 350cc home in the Senior T.T. when finishing thirty-second. Considering the trauma in getting to the Island and the subsequent mechanical problems with the bikes, the 1985 T.T. still provided valuable experience of racing over the Mountain Circuit. This helped him to secure the 125cc and 250cc Irish Road Racing Championships of that year.

Intensive Care

Robert turned his attention to the Formula Two World Championship in 1986 with the view of contesting all the

F

Rob Fisher.

Having a successful T.T. career is every road racer's aim. To win the Newcomer's Race Award is the dream start. Rob Fisher, a former GP rider and British Champion did this in 1993 with a 5th place . . . but the Cumbrian amazed everyone the following year with a record-breaking double, a feat he repeated in 1995 on his Yamaha powered outfit. Few men have achieved so much in so little time. Another victory followed in 1997; he's now chasing the record of nine victories held by Schauzu, Boddice and Saville.

Rob Fisher   Courtesy Peter Wilcock

rounds. The first round would be the T.T. followed by rounds at Jerez in Spain, the Ulster Grand Prix and at Hockenheim in West Germany. The latter was cancelled shortly before the T.T. leaving just the three rounds. Riding a 347cc Dundee Yamaha he qualified fifteenth fastest

**1924 - Junior
Jimmy Simpson
(A.J.S.)
First 60 mph Lap**

on the Island, with a lap of 104.53 mph seventy one seconds down on John Weedon who was quickest.

Mist over the Mountain and light rain lead to a one hour postponement of the Formula Two Race, but by the time the race got underway the sun was out and a strong breeze was drying the roads. The riders were warned that there would still be damp patches under the trees and to ride with caution. Not withstanding this, Robert Dunlop's opening lap was 33.8 seconds faster than his best practice time, with an average speed of 107.32 mph. This put him in fourth place 26.6 seconds behind race leader Brian Reid. Disaster struck thirteen miles into the second lap when Robert crashed at Westwood at over 100 mph. He was helicoptered to hospital with serious leg and chest injuries and placed into intensive care. Brother Joey, who like Robert was due to ride in the Production Race later that day, withdrew his entry and went to his brother's bedside. He said "It wouldn't be right for me to race this afternoon, I am sure the fans will understand". Rothmans Honda Team Manager Barry Symmons fully supported his rider's decision. Joey missed only the Production Race, safe with the knowledge that Robert was not on the danger list. Once out of hospital Robert returned home and enlisted the help of a charm healer to assist with his recovery as he was still troubled by his ankle and shoulder. He was back in the saddle by the 5th of July, coming fifth in the 200cc Race at Skerries.

However his injuries hadn't recovered sufficiently for him to travel to Spain the following week, for the next round of the World Formula Two Championship. He did contest the Ulster Grand Prix, coming tenth in the Formula Two Race.

Fully recovered, after the winter's rest, Robert was fit and raring to go, for what was to be a highly successful, 1987 season. He had bought an ex-Gary Lingham carbon fibre-framed 500cc Suzuki to contest the larger class. Robert achieved a lifetime ambition by beating Joey at the Temple 100 and followed that with victories over him at Mid Antrim and Cookstown. The season finished with Robert taking the Irish and Ulster 125, 350 and 500cc titles as well as being the winner of the prestigious Irish Motorcyclist of the Year Award. As for the T.T. Robert showed no lack of confidence and qualified fifth in

Robert in reflective mood during testing at Jurby Airfield for the 1992 Senior T.T.

Courtesy Mike Hammonds

(Below)
The Hymac Norton of Robert Dunlop at Jurby Airfield

Courtesy Mike Hammonds

the Formula Two with a lap of 108.54 mph, seventh fastest in the Production D at 99.80 mph and fifteenth fastest in the Senior with a lap of 108.75 mph. In the races he retired on the fifth lap in the Junior whilst holding seventh place, having a fastest lap of 108.59 mph. In the Formula Two Race he took his Ken Dundee sponsored Yamaha to fifth place with a race average of 107.50 mph and a fastest lap of 109.39 mph, his quickest to date. The Production D Race gave him a sixth place and his second silver replica of the week, but a broken swinging arm on his R.G. Suzuki made him a non-starter for the Senior Race which was held in the most appalling conditions imaginable.

Record Breaker

Robert, now a full time racer, continued to increase his knowledge in 1988 and set a new personal lap record of 114.54 mph in the Formula One Race and finished sixth in the World Formula One Championship. In early November of that year the 1989 T.T. programme was announced and included the reintroduction of the Ultra Lightweight 125cc class for the first time since Clive Horton won in 1974. Cookstown motor dealer Andy McMenemy provided a 125cc Honda and road haulage contractor P. J. O'Kane a RC30 for the 1989 season.

The lap record for the 125cc race

Robert, on the Hymac Norton, at Parliament Square on his way to third place in the 1992 Senior T.T.
Courtesy Eric Whitehead

(Below Left)
A change of livery in 1993, The Oxford Products Ducati approaching Whitegates.
Courtesy Eric Whitehead

was 100.32 mph set in 1968 by the late Bill Ivy, this was unofficially broken by Robert Dunlop on his second lap in the first practice session on Monday morning 29th

70.43 mph – 1926
Senior
Jimmy Simpson (AJS)
First 70 mph Lap

May. An unofficial record of 100.63 mph was recorded and this was increased to 102.84 mph on Thursday afternoon, giving Robert a 12.8 second advantage over Ian Lougher. Joey Dunlop did not compete in this year's T.T. having not recovered from injuries sustained at Brands Hatch on Good Friday. The two lap Ultra Lightweight Race was held on the morning of Monday 5th June and Robert Dunlop recorded his first T.T. victory when he lead from start to finish. The flying Irishman set new lap and race records in finishing fifteen seconds ahead of Lougher with Carl Fogarty in third. The lap record was raised to 103.02 mph and the race average was 102.58 mph in a time of 44 minutes 08 seconds. This was the first two lap 125cc race since Cecil Sandford won on a M.V. in 1952. Typically, Robert dedicated his race victory to his wife who supported him through the hard times. The T.T. finished with a seventh place in the Formula One Race with a fastest lap of 118.07 mph and fourth in the Senior, gaining two silver replicas. The season ended with him taking third place in the Formula One World Championship behind champion Fogarty and Steve Hislop. This result elevated Robert to top of the Irish grading list for the Formula One World Cup in 1990.

A 'Works' Ride

The continued progress and development of the diminutive Ulsterman had not gone unnoticed and he was offered a

The Medd Honda RC 45 machines of Michael Rutter and Robert Dunlop in the parc-ferme prior to the 1994 Formula One T.T.
Courtesy Mike Hammonds

'works' contract with the J.P.S. Norton Team to compete at the pure road circuits of the North West 200, the T.T. and the Ulster Grand Prix. A damp and bitterly cold Snetterton in early March was where he made his debut ride. Unfortunately it wasn't the start he had wished for, he fell off at the extremely tight Russell's chicane and broke his right collarbone. A successful training session at the same track in early April proved his fitness and suitability to ride the bike. The County Antrim rider repaid the confidence that the Norton Team had in him by winning both his rides at the North West 200 in record breaking time, setting a new outright

lap record in the process. He also won the inaugural 125cc Race showing what a fantastic and versatile rider he is.

The five foot four inch Ulsterman weighing just nine stone set the third fastest lap in practice for the Formula One T.T. with a speed of 119.74 mph, a personal best. He also topped the 125 Ultra Lightweight leaderboard with a lap of 22 minutes 01 seconds a speed of 102.82 mph. The Formula One and 125cc Races were both held on Saturday 2nd June and would test the versatility and stamina of the tiny Irishman. The 125cc Race had been rescheduled from its original Friday evening start. A fast and consistent ride in the Formula One Race brought a well deserved third place behind winner Fogarty and Nick Jefferies, although the race did take its toll. The Norton rider admitted at the finish that the bike was a handful and after six laps he had the blisters to prove it. Less than ninety minutes later the 125cc Race commenced with Dunlop firm favourite on the O'Kane Honda. The race went true to form with the Patsy O'Kane rider winning in record breaking time and at the finish described the difference between the two bikes: "the little Honda appears slow compared with the Norton, you are waiting for the corners to arrive. I did get a little cramp near the end but nothing to worry about."

Preparations for the 1991 T.T. were hampered when the J.P.S. Norton rider broke his collarbone a couple of weeks before the event. To be able to ride the bone had to be plated and the nerves anaesthetised to ease the pain. The pressure on the upper arm, shoulder and collarbone in handling the Norton was too great and the plucky Irishman had to retire in both the Formula One and Senior Races. Although troubled by the discomfort it did not affect his riding on the smaller 125 and 250cc machines. Another record breaking ride in the Ultra-Lightweight Race brought Robert his third consecutive 125cc victory. He set a new lap record of 106.71 mph and a race record of 103.68 mph and denied brother Joey of equalling Mike Hailwood's record of fourteen T.T. wins. It was alleged that he achieved this victory whilst wearing his wife's underwear!! Riding Ray Cowles' 250cc machine in the Junior T.T. gave the likeable Ulsterman his second victory of the week and it was the first time the 125/250cc double had been achieved since Mike Hailwood in 1961.

The following year brother Joey turned the tables and beat Robert into second place in the 125cc Race taking his lap and race records as well. Brian Reid and runner up Steve Hislop pushed the Ray Cowles rider back into third place in the Junior Race. His Norton expired on the second lap of the Formula One Race but gave him the final rostrum position in the Senior T.T. This race took him past the exclusive 120 mph barrier which he broke four times, the fastest being 121.53 mph on the second lap and placed him fifth fastest rider of all time. The demise of Norton opened the door for the charismatic Dunlop to join the Oxford Products Team to race their 888cc Ducati in 1993.

The build up to the T.T. could hardly have gone better with three wins in the smaller classes at the North West 200 and two runner-up places in the Superbike Races behind Fogarty. Practice week went according to plan up until Friday evening, when he crashed exiting Ramsey Hairpin and was helicoptered to Nobles Hospital for a check up. He was later released with heavy bruising to his ribs and hips but fortunately with no broken bones. The big Ducati proved too much to handle in the Formula One Race and a near tearful Dunlop threw in the towel at the end of the fourth lap. Riding with three disposable nappies strapped across his chest the Ultra Lightweight Race was less of a strain although he had difficulty in getting tucked in. The result mirrored the previous year with brother Joey taking the honours

and beating Mike Hailwood's record of T.T. victories. A rostrum position appeared on the cards in the Junior T.T. until a plug lead came off and forced Robert to stop at Ballaugh on the last lap, dropping him to tenth at the finish. Fuel starvation problems with the Ducati caused his retirement on the first lap of the Senior.

Lucky To Be Alive

The 1994 season brought another change with Robert signing for the Medd Racing Team to ride their Honda RC45 machines. A double Superbike victory at the North West 200 plus winning the 125cc Race boosted the Irishman's confidence of doing well on the Isle of Man. Practice went well on the Island with the Medd Honda qualifying third fastest at 120.69 mph in the Formula One, Dunlop's Padgett 250cc Honda was second fastest for the Junior at 115.64 mph and he topped the Ultra Lightweight leader board with a lap of 106.88 mph. Saturday's Formula One Race was started in far from ideal conditions and the diminutive

70.28 mph – 1928
Alec Bennett
(Velocette)
First 70 mph
Junior T.T.

The modified P. J. O'Kane 125cc Honda in the parc ferme before the 1997 Ultra Lightweight Race, note the lack of a front brake lever.

Courtesy Mike Hammonds

Dunlop completed the first lap in sixth place at only 88.73 mph. Conditions were considerably worse than at the Start and many riders pulled in at the end of the first lap. Ironically the weather was improving rapidly as Course Officials decided to stop the race at the end of the second lap. The unofficial winner was Welshman Nigel Davies with Robert in eighth place with a second lap speed of 81.80 mph and a race average of 85.12 mph!!

The race was held the following day in much improved conditions, all of the original field were allowed to start as the first race was declared null and void. The Medd rider quickly settled into the race and held third position for the first three laps, 21.2 seconds behind Phillip McCallen and 4.6 seconds in front of a hard charging Steve Ward. Disaster struck nearly half way round the fourth lap, as Dunlop accelerated out of Ballaugh the back wheel of his Honda collapsed and he was thrown into a wall at over 120 mph. He was helicoptered to hospital with serious injuries, sustaining complicated multiple fractures to right arm and leg. Following the crash the Medd racing team issued this statement:

"Following the serious incident regarding our number one rider Robert Dunlop in yesterday's

Formula One Race, the team have made a decision to withdraw from the 1994 T.T. It is with the greatest respect to Robert that whilst he fights to save his career the whole team give him total support. With regard to the incident I would like to confirm that there was no rider error involved, the accident was caused by a component failure . . ." Stuart Medd, Team Manager.

Triumphant Return

Multiple operations and a lengthy recuperation period followed but the will to race again never diminished. The legacy of the accident was that he was unable to use his right hand and had severely restricted movement in his right arm. In order to race again he needed to modify any bike he was to ride by using a special thumb-operated brake lever mounted on the left handlebar. After two years the courageous Dunlop started to race again in the 125cc class. His entry for the 1996 North West 200 was refused but was accepted by the A.C.U. for the T.T. provided he passed a medical. He arrived on the Island for the T.T. but, unfortunately, did not pass his medical and could not race. Undeterred, he carried on improving his fitness at home and once again entered the North West 200 and the T.T. in 1997. Having proved his fitness by racing in Ireland the A.C.U. accepted his entry for the T.T. allowing him to race with the uniquely modified braking system on his bike. Strangely, the North West 200

Robert Dunlop in the paddock before the 1998 Ultra-Lightweight T.T.
Courtesy Albert Cooper, The Mirror

committee felt that it could be dangerous and refused his entry.

Monday 26th May saw Robert Dunlop make an emotional return to the Mountain Circuit when he completed two laps on his 125cc O'Kane Honda, the first at 88.92 mph and the second at 102.99 mph putting him third fastest. Asked if he was nervous going through Ballaugh he said "No, I didn't give it a thought, the accident wasn't rider error and therefore I had nothing to fear." He finished the week fifth fastest with a lap of 106.97 mph set on Thursday afternoon. The week

wasn't without its trauma when he lost the feeling in his left hand, he said " I started to get pins and needles in my left hand as I came out of Ramsey, so I had to take my hand off the bars and shake it." It was discovered that his leathers were too tight and this restricted the blood flow. Race day didn't bring the fairy tale victory that the fans wanted but a magnificent ride gave the ever popular Irishman third position and a place on the rostrum. The result finally silenced his detractors. Robert's race average was 107.14 mph with a fastest lap of 108.41 mph. Fittingly the race was won by Ian Lougher who was on the rostrum with Robert back in 1983.

Robert's rehabilitation continued throughout the season and included 125cc victories at Scarborough, Aberdare, Fore, the Southern 100, Monaghan and Mid-Antrim. He also appeared to have patched up his differences with Billy Nutt, when his entry was accepted for the Ulster Grand Prix. Unfortunately the race didn't go to plan, a rain interrupted race ended when his Honda seized, at Deers Leap.

Billy Nutt and the North West 200

76.28 mph – 1930
Senior
Wal Handley (Rudge)
First Lap
under 30 minutes

Committee now agreed that Robert and his modified breaking system were safe and accepted his entry for the 125cc event at the 1998 North West 200. It was a decision that Robert nearly didn't live to regret. In a race that was restarted twice and eventually abandoned, Robert crashed twice. The second of which he was lucky to survive, on approaching University Corner his right arm was pulled off the handle bars by Davy Lemon who collided into him. Robert lost control and was thrown over the top of his bike into a signpost and landed back into the road. All who witnessed this, feared the worst, but he was lucky to escape with fractures to his collarbone and the tibia of his right leg. Practice for the T.T. was only a fortnight away and there seemed little, to no chance, of the P. J. O'Kane rider being able to travel to the Island.

Speculation was rife on the Island as to whether either of the Dunlop brothers would be fit enough to ride, Joey having broken his hand and having part of a finger amputated after a crash at Tandragee in early May.

Joey was passed fit but decided to compete only on his 125cc and 250cc machines, feeling that the larger machines were too big to hold on to. Robert didn't travel to the Island until the Monday of practice week, arriving at Ronaldsway Airport on crutches. He had a medical that afternoon and was confident of passing, declaring "I hope to ride with a lightweight cast on my leg. The gear change system is on the left of the bike, I only need my right leg to support myself." He successfully passed his medical but decided not to practice that evening. Tuesday evening's practice was cancelled due to poor weather and Robert had decided not to participate in any of the early morning practice sessions. Wednesday evening was the first time he was able to ride and he completed two laps, the first of which was at a gingerly 99.93 mph followed by a heartening lap of 106.17 mph. Another two laps were completed in the Thursday afternoon practice session with a fastest lap of 107.61 mph which left the diminutive Irishman quite contented, albeit a little uncomfortable. The final practice session of the week saw Robert once again complete two laps, one of which he would not have foreseen even in his wildest dreams. He lapped in 20 minutes 24.7 seconds at an average speed of 110.91 mph - an incredible 18.5 seconds inside Ian Lougher's lap record - and 42.1 seconds faster than Gary Dynes who finished second fastest on the practice leader board.

(Top)
The victorious Dunlop on the rostrum after the Ultra-Lightweight 1998 T.T.
Courtesy Albert Cooper, The Mirror

Robert crossing the line to win the 1998 Ultra -Lightweight.
Courtesy Albert Cooper, The Mirror

Robert accelerating away from the Gooseneck on his way to the final rostrum position in his remarkable come back race.

Courtesy Eric Whitehead

G

Glen Helen.

The Glen was developed in 1850 by a Mr. Marsden and named after his daughter. Its focal point was the Swiss Chalet; thousands of trees were planted on the valley sides and along the banks of the River Neb. Soon becoming a tourist honey-pot for vistors and locals alike, it is now one of the most dramatic vantage points on the T.T. Course. Enthusiasts sit on the bank, watch the riders approach along the twisty section from Ballig Bridge and then climb up Creg Willey's to Sarah's Cottage. Now the site of a radio commentary box, Glen Helen is situated 10 miles from the start.

How idyllic - watching your favourite sport with a pint in hand!
Courtesy FoTTofinders Archive Research System

Honda's One Hundredth Victory

The Manx weather played havoc with the 1998 T.T. Race Programme, with all but the final days races being affected. The Ultra-Lightweight Race was due to be held on Wednesday June 10th over four laps of the Mountain Course, but this was reduced to three laps half an hour before the race was due to start. The starting time was brought forward by the organisers in an attempt to beat another bout of rain that was heading towards the Island.

The weather conditions were very unpredictable and tyre choice would be crucial to the outcome of the race, which was started with drying roads from a very blustery wind. Many riders chose a combination of intermediates or cut slicks but the determined younger Dunlop gambled with slick tyres front and back. Brother Joey went for cut slicks and this gave Robert some food for thought at the start as Joey rarely makes a mistake with his tyre choice. He need not have worried, for the race could not have gone better for Robert as he lead from start to finish. He had been chased by Gavin Lee for the first two laps but he retired at the Pits at the end of the second and this elevated Ian Lougher into the runners up spot. Lougher had used a legally oversized tank to avoid having to a have a pit stop and had moved up from sixth position at the end of lap two with a last lap of 107.53 mph., the fastest of the race. Robert had a comfortable 17.9 seconds cushion at the end of the race and a winning average speed of 106.38 mph. The reception Robert received, for his fifth T.T. victory, was tremendous and there could not have been a more popular winner. He said "My tyre choice paid off as the only rain I encountered was on the second lap from the Mountain Mile until the Bungalow, other than that it was dry roads all the way except for the odd damp patch. My injuries are fine

H

Helicopter.

On Lap 3 of the 1963 250cc Race Tony Godfrey crashed at Milntown sustaining serious head injuries. He became the first rider to be airlifted to Nobles Hospital, Douglas, by rescue helicopter. He eventually recovered from his injuries sufficiently to race again on the Mountain Course. In 1997 the special ambulance-fit French Aero-Spatiale Twin Squirrel Aircraft, running on Jet AI fuel, similar to paraffin or kerosene, averaged a record 13.3 minutes from the alert of an accident to landing the injured competitor at Ballakermeen School Fields, 90 seconds ambulance drive from the hospital.

The helicopter lifts off on its maiden trip - to airlift Tony Godfrey to hospital in the 1963 Lightweight 250cc T.T.
Courtesy FoTTofinders Archive Research System

although the ligaments are now stiffening up." The Prize Presentation was held at the Villa Marina that evening and Robert received another standing ovation, he tossed his crutches into the crowd to show that he didn't really need them, to more thunderous applause.

It wasn't recognised at the time, but Robert Dunlop not only won his fifth T.T. but also Honda's "one hundredth" T.T. victory in the Honda Corporation's Fiftieth Anniversary year. The press reported it as Honda's ninety-eighth victory but the official Honda victory list failed to include the ten lap 500cc Production T.T. wins of 1975 and 1976. These Class

victories, like Paul Williams's 1998 400cc win, were achieved on Hondas by Charlie Williams and Eddie Roberts in 1975 and by Frank Rutter and Mick Poxon in 1976. The races being 'Le Mans' start two-man team events. The prestige and honour of gaining Honda's one hundredth victory is one Robert Dunlop richly deserved.

Motorcycle road racers are renowned for being a hardy breed but Robert Dunlop stands alone when it comes to triumphing over adversity. He is a beacon for anybody to follow with his courage, tenacity, determination and willingness to succeed.

80.92 mph – 1931
Senior
**Jimmy Simpson
(Norton)
First 80 mph lap**

The first lap of the ill-fated 1994 Formula One T.T., the Medd Honda rounding Quarter Bridge.
Courtesy Mike Hammonds

Tiddlers at the T.T.

Only two years after the Ultra-Lightweight 125cc Class returned to the Mountain Course it was joined by even smaller capacity machines - the 50cc tiddlers. Keeping apace with the Grand Prix scene the T.T. Organisers introduced the two lap event to supplement the traditional Senior Race Day programme.

The British 50cc scene was dominated by the Italian Itom machine with its high pitched whining engine revving up to

(Right)
1962 50cc T.T. – Ernst Degner (Suzuki) starts his victorious race.
(Below)
Dan Shorey (II Kreidler) and Mitsuo Itoh (Suzuki) push their bikes into action (1962).

12,000rpm. However, it was totally outclassed at the T.T. by factory Suzukis, Hondas and Kreidlers with their multi-speed gearboxes.

As the grid assembled on Glencrutchery Road on that Friday

90.27 mph – 1937
Senior
**Freddie Frith (Norton)
First 90 mph lap**

31

RM62 Suzuki which was faster and handled better than the equally diminutive Honda. Honda actually had to cable home for ten-speed gear boxes to replace the eight which the company thought would be competitive. Amazingly, these were made, flown to the Island and fitted in time for the race. Unfortunately, for them, Taveri and Robb trailed the German with Hans Georg Anscheidt bringing his 12-speed Kreidler home in 4th position. Minter (Honda) was 9th and Shorey (Kreidler) 11th. Beryl Swain riding with no fairing finished a creditable twenty-second out of the twenty-five who completed the course.

Bryans (Honda) leads Morishita (Suzuki) over Ballaugh Bridge on their way to 2nd and 3rd places respectively in 1964.

Short circuit single-cylinder specialist, Derek Minter tries his hand at 50cc racing. He finished 9th in the inaugural race on his Honda

German, Degner lead from start to finish to average 75.12 mph on his

morning in June there was another notable T.T. First . . . Mrs. Beryl Swain, astride her Itom became the first lady solo competitor. Among the 57 entries were a clutch of Japanese riders, Itoh, Ichino, Shimazaki and Suzuki ideally suited to the small machines, but also stalwarts of the British scene such as Derek Minter and Dan Shorey, normally seen on larger single cylinder machinery. However, the race was dominated by seasoned Continental Circus competitors Ernst Degner, Luigi Taveri and Tommy Robb. East

Prior to 1962 Degner had been a works rider for the East German MZ concern, but after the '61 Swedish Grand Prix he disappeared and escaped to seek asylum in West Germany, his wife and two children having gone ahead. At the time he was very much in contention with Australian Tom Phillis (Honda) for the 125cc World Championship. Degner had no MZ for the final race in Argentina, but was offered an EMC designed by Joe Ehrlich and backed by the De Havilland Aircraft firm. The jilted East Germans were naturally furious and so suspended Degner's competition licence. After much discussion he was not allowed to ride; Phillis duly won the race and title but Degner joined the Suzuki concern for the following season, taking many MZ mechanical secrets with him.

Rather than suffer another

humiliation Honda decided not to enter the 50cc class in 1963 allowing Suzuki with their engine now sporting a rear-facing exhaust,

The 1965 Honda RC 115 twin as seen at the Honda 50th anniversary celebrations, 1998.
Courtesy Albert Cooper, The Mirror

new 24mm carburettor and nine-speed gearbox to dominate proceedings. The race, increased to three laps, was lead by Degner until

I

Steve Ives.

In 1990 the top short circuit competitor tackled the T.T. Course for the first time. This was a learning year, with sights set on a 100mph lap ... a feat achieved by the end of Practice Week. However, life on the world's longest course was not without incident as Steve explained at the time: "I was coming out of Quarry Bends, flat on the tank with the 250 Kawasaki revving at over 12,000 when all of a sudden this old guy walked out in front of me with a kettle in his hand. He obviously hadn't noticed me as he was looking straight ahead trying not to spill any water. I came out of the bubble, banged my foot on the floor, wobbled all over the place, but managed to keep control."

80.44 mph – 1949
Dickie Dale
(Guzzi)
First 80 mph lap
– 250 T.T.

A massed start for the 1996 event. . . Bryans (1) and Taveri (2), both Honda finished in that order. Giving chase from the onset were the Suzukis of Anderson (3), Ansheidt (7) and Smith (15).

his machine expired on the last lap allowing Mitsuo Itoh to head home his Suzuki team mate, New Zealander Hugh Anderson, by 27 seconds. Degner did have the honour of raising the lap record to 79.10 mph. Itoh is of course, so far, the only Japanese rider to win a T.T. race, but the most telling factor was that only eight competitors finished. Surely the 50cc race could not be in decline already? Of the eight, there were four Suzukis, one Kreidler, that of Anscheidt in third, less than five seconds behind Anderson, a Honda, a Tomatsu and a Sheene Special in seventh with a young Bill Ivy aboard.

Honda returned in 1964 with

Ralph Bryans and Japanese ace Taniguchi; Taveri having joined Anscheidt and Tarquino Provini on Kreidlers. However, for the third year running, a Suzuki rider took the laurels. This time it was the man from Auckland, Hugh Anderson, surely the tallest man to win an International 50cc race. Anderson first came to Europe in 1960 with a 7R AJS and a 500cc Manx Norton; a string of steady placings brought him to the notice of factory teams, but any 'promotion' had to be delayed until 1962 due to an

accident at the '61 Dutch T.T.. The likeable Antipodean retired at the end of the 1966 season, concerned at the high accident rate among riders, to run a motor cycle business. He, of course, returned to the racing scene in the 1980's campaigning his immaculate G50 Matchless in Classic events.

Anderson led the three lap '64 Tiddler T.T. from start to finish creating a new lap record of 81.13mph. Starting Number 3 he soon overtook Anscheidt and Koshino (Suzuki) to lead on the roads, but a fair old battle went on

Beryl Swain, Itom, at the bottom of Bray Hill. *Courtesy FoTTofinders Archive Research System*

J

Jubilee T.T. 1977

To celebrate the 25th anniversary of Queen Elizabeth II a one-off race for solo machines was held on the final day of the week. Sponsored by Schweppes, the four lap Jubilee T.T. provided a young Ulsterman by the name of Joey Dunlop with his first victory. Riding a Yamaha he led home George Fogarty, father of Carl, and Steve Tonkin.

behind him. Itoh was second at the end of the first lap, but dropped to 5th at the chequered flag; Anscheidt took over his mantle on the second circuit only to drop to 4th; Ralph Bryans with a final lap spurt leapt from 5th to 2nd. Although Honda did not win, the factory was pleased that five of its newly developed CR 110s finished, winning two replicas.

After a short delay the 1965 Race was run in rain squalls and gale force winds which all but blew riders off the road. Honda had developed a fast, reliable twin cylinder machine; so to combat this, Suzuki designed the impressive RK65 water cooled twin with a twelve speed gearbox, alleged to produce 16hp at 16,500 rpm. Despite this, practice performance indicated that Bryans and Taveri, now back with the Japanese marque, were favourites. Bryans, who unofficially broke the lap record during training, however, stopped at Quarter Bridge soon after starting to change plugs on his nine speed machine. He got no further than the Gooseneck on Lap 2. Itoh led after the first 37¾ miles, but he departed the fray at Greeba Castle with engine trouble after spending a lengthy pit stop at the end of lap 2, leaving Taveri to win his third T.T. by 53 secs from Anderson. Fitted with unusual cross-over exhausts, the Swiss rider's little twin ran at 20,000 rpm. Degner was third, but these three factory riders were so far ahead of Charlie Mates' Honda that no bronze replicas were awarded. Of the 28 starters, only 10 finished, with the last three of these being

flagged off at Governor's Bridge to avoid delaying the start of the Senior. Ian Plumridge in fifth was racing one of the Spanish Derbi machines that had been offered to a handful of riders to run on a private basis. One notable absentee was Anscheidt; after disastrous results at early continental Grand Prix Kreidler withdrew their machines leaving their number one rider to join Suzuki for the 1966 season.

1966 saw the fastest ever 50cc lap - 85.66 mph by Ralph Bryans in winning the three lap event. Even the massed start, employed for the first time in this event, failed to produce any really exciting moments in this rather dull but record-breaking race. Although only 17 men started the race the noise of the predominantly Japanese engined field was tremendous as they headed towards the top of Bray Hill. Suzuki, who had done some development to produce a gear box containing 14 ratios instead of 12 with a power output lifted to 18hp at 17,500 rpm, was no match for Honda. Bryans and Taveri were one and two respectively for the entire

91.38 mph – 1951 Geoff Duke (Norton) First 90 mph lap – Junior T.T.

race with Anderson moving from fifth on lap one to take the final rostrum place at the finish. The whole of the field completed the first lap - a rare achievement in TT racing up to this point; in fact, only four retired in the whole race. The only anxious moment for Bryans was when the motor cut out on the last lap at Creg-ny-Baa, only to cut back in again rounding Brandish corner.

An interesting finisher in twelfth place, aboard a Honda, was Alan Robinson riding in his only T.T. race. Alan now organises the annual Classic Parade in which he is always the last solo participant to start so that, as he says, "I can check that all my friends are safely round the T.T. course."

Honda withdrew from the 50cc and 125cc classes for 1967, leaving the way open for a Suzuki walkover in the race that had 24 starters. However, team orders were to play a part . . . apparently, Anscheidt was

scheduled to win the World Championship, but Katayama the T.T. with Anscheidt second and Stuart Graham third. Anscheidt and Graham headed the field after the massed start, but were caught by the Japanese rider at Ramsey where they duly upped the pace. The three rode line astern until the Verandah on lap two when Katayama looked over his shoulder to see where his team mates were, only to lose concentration and drive into a ditch. Although unhurt he was out of the race; the Cheshire rider gradually pulled away from Anscheidt to win by 9 seconds. This was against team orders, but factory bosses were pleased because a victory by the son of T.T. legend Les Graham on one of their machines gave them good publicity. Irishman Tommy Robb, also on a Suzuki, finished third, nearly ten minutes adrift.

It was Australian Barrie Smith who, after Japanese withdrawal from the 50cc World Championship, won the last 50cc T.T. on a factory Derbi in 1968. After team mate Angel Nieto dropped his machine, Smith deliberately slowed down to give the others a chance of gaining a replica winning at an average speed of 72.90 mph. He finished with a lead of nearly three minutes from the Hondas of Chris Walpole and Les Griffiths. Griffiths, from Bristol and 54 years of age became, and remains, the oldest solo competitor to mount the T.T. rostrum on Glencrutchery Road.

And so 50cc racing on the Mountain Course came to an end although it continued as a World

K

Peter Kneale.

Peter Kneale is widely considered to be the "Voice of the T.T." A marshal since 1949, Peter moved into the Time Box as an auditor in 1963 and then made the first live Manx Radio broadcast in 1965 from a small cramped box near the start line on the inside of the course. Sometime later he moved into the main Grandstand where he has a prime view of the start-finish line to give his know-ledgeable, in-depth commentaries. In 1984 Peter took over as Press Officer for the races and in 1999 succeeded former A-CU Chairman, the late Vernon Cooper, as President of the T.T. Supporters' Club.

Peter Kneale

L

Heinz Luthringshauser.

This popular Sidecar driver from Germany first competed in the T.T. in 1961 when he finished 11th. Always on BMW machinery, he proved to be a remarkably consistent finisher - fifth in '62, fourth in '65, third in both '68 and '70 and runner-up in '72. 1974 proved to be the icing on the cake - second in Race One, followed by that elusive victory later in the week. Heinz Luthringshauser is still the only rider to win a T.T. race having an artificial leg!

Heinz Luthringshauser, BMW.

Championship until 1983 when it was replaced the following year by the 80cc Class. Statistically, a review of 50cc racing at the T.T. is quite interesting. The seven race series threw up seven different winners - five from overseas, one Irishman, but only one, Stuart Graham, from England. On only two occasions did the T.T. winner go on to win that year's World Championship - Degner in '62 and Anderson in '64. The fastest lap was made by the winner each year except 1963 when Ernst Degner eclipsed any time Mitsuo Itoh could muster. In terms of consistency Hugh Anderson came out on top with four top three placings, which is amazing considering his height; Luigi Taveri had three rostrum placings. Only three makes of machines were victorious - Suzuki(4), Honda(2) and Barry Smith's Derbi. This was Derbi's only T.T. victory and the class provided Kreidler with its only top three placing. Although, with the exception of 1962, they were poorly supported races in terms of entries the spectators did see some close on-the-road racing and glimpsed exotic machinery which made an interesting comparison with the British single cylinder machinery of the day.

95.22 mph – 1951
Senior
Geoff Duke (Norton)
First 95 mph lap

KLAUS KLEIN
More than just a road racer

Klaus Klein`s 20th and final T.T. Race took place on Saturday 6th June 1987 in the most appalling weather conditions. The race had been postponed from the previous day due to the bad weather and was held on the Saturday in torrential rain and high blustery winds; these were the worst conditions that race winner Joey Dunlop had ever experienced. Klaus finished the four lap race in 18th position having dropped down the leader board when his Bimota Yamaha started to misfire. When interviewed after the race he described the conditions as "the worst I have ever known but I have been soaked every night this week at the Palace Lido judging the Miss Wet T.T-Shirt competition, so I do not suppose that it matters that I get soaked on the race track as well!!" Without doubt Klaus Klein was a self confessed T.T. fanatic and a fans favourite, he mixed freely with the race fans and participated actively in as many aspects of the T.T. Festival that racing commitments would allow. He was held with the same regard as those other fun loving riders such as Roger Marshall, Steve Parrish, Charlie

Williams and Barry Woodland, all of whom have delighted the crowds with their dexterity with a soda-syphon !

Fresh from a successful sidecar career, twice being runner up in the West German Championship, Klaus Klein changed direction in 1980 and started to race solo machines. With the help of T.T. stalwart Bill Smith he entered the 1981 Isle of Man T.T. with the intention of riding in the Senior and Classic Races on his 496cc Suzuki. Klaus, a vehicle service manager from Stuttgart, duly arrived on the Isle of Man in May 1981 to make his T.T. debut. That year's T.T. certainly wasn't without incident and controversy, it was the year of the infamous Honda 'Black Bike' protest in the Senior T.T. The protest was over Suzuki's Graeme Crosby elevation from third to first place and thus depriving Honda's Ron Haslam of victory.

The Senior T.T. was due to start at 11 o'clock on Monday 8th June but was delayed by one hour due to the inclement Manx weather. The race did commence at noon in what can only be described as poor conditions with Klaus 51st on the grid. The race

was barely a lap old when the Clerk of the Course decided that conditions had deteriorated to such an extent that the race would be stopped at the end of the second lap. Chris Guy had lead the race for the two laps and was less than amused that the race had been stopped and the result was null and void. Riding with race number 13 certainly didn't bring Chris any luck that day or when the race was re-run the following day. He was caught out by a shower of rain at Braddan Bridge on the fifth lap and crashed out of the race, fortunately without injury. Klaus rode a steady race to finish his first T.T. in 18th place with a race average speed of 99.08 mph winning a much cherished and well earned bronze replica. Mick Grant won the race with a start to finish victory on his Suzuki. The Classic Race was run in near perfect conditions and was notable for being the first six lap T.T. to be won in under two hours ! Klaus finished in a very credible 13th place with a race average speed of 104.90 mph winning another bronze replica.

The 1982 season saw Klaus join forces with twice ex-world

champion and former T.T. winner Dieter Braun with the aim of contesting selected Grand Prix Races, the European 500cc Championship, the German National Championship and the Isle of Man T.T. He entered three T.T.'s, the Senior and Classic Races on his 496cc Suzuki and the Formula Two on a 550cc Kawasaki.

The Senior Race ended in bitter disappointment at Union Mills on the second lap when his Suzuki seized, however the Formula Two brought some success with eleventh place at a speed of 94.89 mph gaining another bronze replica. The seized engine gave Klaus and his mechanics much work to do before it would be ready for the Friday's Classic Race. The engine was rebuilt through the night prior to the race and, as such, there had been no time to test it properly before scrutineering. It was a rather apprehensive Klein who pushed his bike to the start line, but in true T.T. fashion he need not have worried. The bike didn't miss a beat throughout the race although he did have problems with the chain that persisted in jumping the sprocket for the last couple of laps. Despite this trouble, Klaus moved from ninth position at the end of lap four to finish the race in a fantastic fourth place, just 7.4 seconds behind third finisher, Tony Rutter. His last lap speed was 107.52 mph and his race average was 105.72 mph in a time of 2 hours 8 minutes 30.2 seconds; commenting on this he said "I thought a top 12 finish might be possible, but fourth is very special.

I've spent all my money on spares after all the trouble I had in practice and in the Senior Race but that was worth it for this result. I had no idea what position I was in because I didn't have anyone signalling for me out on the course, if I had, maybe I could have gone faster and caught Tony Rutter." This was not only his best T.T. result but his finest since turning to solos two years ago.

The 1983 season again saw Klaus teamed up with Dieter Braun following a similar race agenda as the previous year. At the T.T. he entered three events, the 350cc T.T. the Formula Two and the Senior Classic. Racing a 348cc Yamaha he finished 19th in the six lap 350cc T.T. in a race time of 2 hours 14 minutes 39.2 seconds, an average speed of 100.87 mph to gain a

bronze replica. The Formula Two Race was the first time that he had completed a race outside the replica winning time, finishing in 18th

85.52 mph – 1953 Fergus Anderson (Guzzi) First 85 mph lap 250cc T.T.

place in a time of 1 hour 35 minutes 44.6 seconds for the four lap race to gain a finishers award. The success of the previous year could not be repeated in the Senior Classic Race because he retired at the Pits at the end of the third lap when in tenth place. The race wasn't without some satisfaction; he lapped at 111.09 mph on the first circuit which was the fastest he had ever been. Although the T.T. wasn't his most successful, the season ended on a high with Klaus finishing runner up in both the European and German 500cc Championships.

The 1984 season was to be his last with the Dieter Braun Team and he entered three races at the T.T. the Formula One, Senior and Premier Classic. The Formula One race brought disappointment when his 747cc Suzuki expired at Kirk Michael on the fourth lap. The race had been a struggle and he retired whilst holding eleventh place. Klaus had the honour of starting on the front row of the grid and leading the field away in the Senior Race, having been given the prestigious Number One Plate. This honour was something he would keep for the rest of his T.T. career. Unfortunately starting from pole position did not bring the victory that he so dearly yearned. A frantic first lap ended with him in eighth place and a visit to his pit. He had clipped a wall and

damaged the bikes fairing, which had to be made safe. This unscheduled stop dropped him out of contention and his luck eventually ran out on the fourth lap when he retired at Ballacraine. Lady luck had not totally deserted the popular German rider and would shine brightly upon him in the Senior Classic Race. Riding with a broken clutch lever from the third lap he unbelievably repeated his 1982 performance by finishing fourth and gaining another silver replica. This was not his only success; he had arrived on the Island with the ambition of breaking the 114 mph barrier and he achieved this on the second lap with a speed of 114.25 mph. This placed him thirteenth in the all time list of fastest riders one position ahead of the late Mike Hailwood but still four miles an hour down on Joey Dunlop's outright lap record of 118.48 mph. The race was won by Rob McElnea with Joey Dunlop second and Mick Grant third; Klaus's fourth place now put him with the elite of pure road racing.

Riding for 'Team Rally Sport' he entered four races in the 1985 T.T., the World Championship Formula One and Two Races, 750cc Production Race and Senior T.T. This year's T.T. was to prove to be (literally) a very up and down event. Practice week started well with him topping the Senior leader board on Tuesday evening with a lap of 110.93 mph. This speed was increased on Wednesday evening to 111.41 mph when he was second to Roger Marshall, who had lapped at

114.30 mph. Thursday afternoon's practice was to end spectacularly at the 33rd Milestone when he crashed. He lost traction when he hit the oil that Mick Grant's GSX-R Suzuki had left on the road after his engine exploded a few moments earlier. The helicopter was summoned and Klaus was flown to Nobles Hospital for a check up; he was discharged later that afternoon with a clean bill of health. Not to waste much valued practice time Mick Grant hitched a ride in the helicopter back to the Grandstand

Klaus Klein passing through Parliament Square on his way to tenth place, in the reduced to four laps, 1986 Formula 1 T.T.
Courtesy John Burness

and took another bike out for a lap!

Never being one to let things get the better of him, the likeable German was ready and waiting to start the Formula One Race from the front of the grid. The 730cc Suzuki proved to be quite a handful and resulted in another tumble when he slid off at Governors Bridge on the fourth lap whist holding ninth place. Undeterred he picked himself up and continued to eventually finish in sixteenth position in a time of 1 hour 10 minutes 26.2 seconds an average speed of 104.13 mph to win yet another bronze replica. The Formula Two Race brought another low when his Yamaha expired at Ballacraine on the first lap forcing him out of the race. Riding a GSX-R 750 Suzuki Klaus finished the MCN/Avon Tyres Production T.T. in

eleventh position, one place behind a young Steve Hislop and eleven in front of Joey Dunlop, adding another bronze replica to his collection.

A beautiful sunny day dawned on Friday, seventh of June, and conditions for the Senior T.T. would have been perfect had it not been for a very strong blustery wind , which would catch the riders on the more exposed sections of the course. Klaus set off from his now customary Number One spot with Mark Johns along side him. The first lap ended with Klaus lying second on the road and in the race, just 15.2 seconds behind Joey Dunlop, with a speed of 112.95 mph. The following pack was lead by the hard charging Roger Marshall, who claimed second place by the end of lap two, being 7.6 seconds in front of Klein, who, in turn, was just 3.8 seconds ahead of Mark Johns. The leader board changed again by the end of the third lap with Klaus now relegated to fourth, 3.4 seconds behind Sam McClements and 2.6 seconds ahead of Johns. Roger Marshall who had

87.02 mph – 1954
Senior
Alistair King (B.S.A.)
Fastest lap
Clubman T.T.

Klein trying hard at Ramsey in the 1987 Formula 1 T.T.

Courtesy John Burness

started fifty seconds behind the German at the start was now only 14.4 seconds adrift on the road and gaining quickly. Half way round the fourth lap Klaus was in a three-way dice with Johns and Marshall which thrilled the kerbside spectators. The excitement was unfortunately short-lived; Klaus being the German filling in an English sandwich crashed heavily at Glen Tramman right in front of the fast approaching Roger Marshall. Marshall said after the race "I haven't a clue how I missed him or the bike, the back wheel shot up in the air with the force of breaking, I was really lucky." Unfortunately for Klaus he was not so lucky , he broke an ankle, all but destroyed his bike when it caught fire, and was out of racing for the rest of the season. Klaus, however, was not the only racer to take a helicopter ride that day, Mick Grant, his practice flying companion, had crashed at the Black Dub on the second lap and was

flown to hospital for a check up. The irony of Grants crash was that the following rider slipped on the oil left by his bike bringing the rider down. Unfortunately the ill-fated Rob Vine did not have the same luck as Klaus had had at the 33rd Milestone and sustained fatal injuries.

The 1986 season started with another change of livery having gained sponsorship from the German clothing manufacturer, Hein Gericke. Few race fans who saw him will forget the distinctive white helmet, leathers and bike with

the red logo emblazoned on it; it was certainly the smartest in the paddock. Fully recovered from the previous year's crash he returned to the Isle of Man to ride a 749cc Suzuki in the Formula One and Senior Races and a 346cc Yamaha in the Formula Two T.T. Klaus was determined to put the shenanigans of 1985 behind him and strive for a more consistent performance. Practice week started well when he set the third fastest Formula One time of the week on Monday evening with a lap of 20 minutes

24.0 seconds, an average speed of 110.97 mph. Unfortunately for Klaus he could not carry this good form through to the other classes, only managing to qualify seventeenth fastest in the Formula Two with a lap of 103.65 mph. on Wednesday evening and twenty-seventh fastest in the Senior lapping at 103.92 mph on Wednesday morning including a fall at Governors Bridge.

Saturday's World Championship Formula One race was abandoned after several postponements due to the extremely bad weather on the Island and was rescheduled to take place the next day, 'Mad Sunday'. There was no let up in the weather and racing on 'Mad Sunday' was also abandoned and a new race programme was released by the officials, with Saturday's races now taking place on Monday, and Monday's races taking place on Tuesday.

Monday dawned with brighter weather but there was still the possibility of low lying mist over the Mountain. The race did however get away on time at 11.30am with Klaus leading the field away with Brian Reid adjacent. Wary of previous postponements and the unpredictability of the Manx weather the Stewards reduced the length of the race from six to four laps. At the end of the first lap Klaus was fourth to cross the line, however he was only in eleventh position on corrected time. He maintained this position for the next two laps and eventually finished in tenth place in a time of 1 hour 23 minutes 29.2 seconds averaging 108.46 mph. This was 3

minutes 19.8 seconds behind race winner Joey Dunlop. Tuesday's World Championship Formula Two Race was also subject to a reduced race distance by two laps and a delayed start by one hour. The four lap race eventually got underway but the conditions were only moderate when Klaus Klein and Steve Cull were flagged away from the start and accelerated towards the top of Bray Hill. This was not to be a happy race for the West German because he was well down on time at the first commentary point at Ballacraine and was then reported to have fallen off at the Gooseneck. He remounted and continued but, not surprisingly, pulled into the Pits at the end of the lap and retired. Asked about his problems a

99.97 mph – 1955
Senior
Geoff Duke
(Gilera)
So near yet so far!

dejected Klein said "The bike was wrongly geared and going much too slow and if that was not enough I was knocked off it at the Gooseneck. I moved over to let someone go by when the ******* went the other side and knocked me off."

The Senior Race Day was notable for three things, firstly it was bright and sunny, secondly the front row of the grid was filled by two West German riders and thirdly the race was flagged away by His Royal Highness the Duke of Kent. Klaus and Helmut Dahne led the large field away and by the end of the lap he was amongst the leading riders on the road but was well down on corrected time. His opening lap of 109.92 mph was four miles per hour slower than race leader Roger Marshall and left him in a lowly thirteenth position. He battled gainfully against his ailing Suzuki but failed to make any impression and eventually retired on lap five at Kirk Michael Police Station. It had been a troubled race, not least his second lap pit stop where his pit crew spilt petrol over the rear wheel causing the scrutineers to delay his departure.

In what turned out to be the last time Klaus would ride on the Isle of Man he again wore the distinctive Hein Gericke colours for the 1987 T.T. He rode in just two events, the World Championship Formula One and the Senior T.T. on a FZR 750 Yamaha. Once again he had the prestigious Number One plate and lead the F1 field away. Although he was not up with the leaders he held a consistent top ten position throughout until electrical problems forced his retirement on the last lap. He crossed the line in seventh place at the end of the fifth lap but had to stop at Greeba Castle to make adjustments. He continued but was forced to retire a few hundred yards down the road at the Hawthorne Inn, an appropriate place for the fun loving Klein!

Klaus Klein's final T.T. Race was held on Saturday 6th June 1987 in the most appalling weather conditions. The race had already been postponed from the previous day along with the Production 'A' and 'C' races. Klaus and Geoff Johnson lead the field away in treacherous conditions for the shortened four lap event. The race was notable for the courage shown by all the riders for attempting to race in the most atrocious conditions imaginable. The race was won by Joey Dunlop in record breaking time!! However the race record for a four lap Senior T.T. was held by Ray Amm from 1954, which was the last time it was reduced from six laps. For the record Klaus toured in to finish eighteenth in a time of 1 hour 40 minutes 01.6 seconds an average speed of 90.52 mph gaining his final bronze replica. The worsening weather conditions meant the cancellation of the Production Races, the first time that a T.T. Race had not been run.

The poor Manx weather was repeated in Northern Ireland in August of 1987 when the Ulster Grand Prix was due to be run. In a routine familiar to T.T. riders the Formula One Race at Dundrod was delayed by one hour on Saturday 15th August due to a torrential down-pour. Course officials deemed that after this delay the conditions had improved sufficiently to allow racing to commence, some riders did however ask for a further delay but this request was turned down.

The race began with surface water on the track, the riders crossed the start and finish line at the end of the first lap in a shower of spray. Joey Dunlop was in fifth position with Klaus right behind him in sixth, as Klaus hurtled past the pits he tried to change into top gear with disastrous consequences. When engaging top gear the bike skidded and Klaus was thrown into the hedgerow at a speed in excess of 100 mph killing him instantly. Tragically, Klaus's father had witnessed the crash from the start area and in that moment he lost his son and 'Pure Road Racing' lost one of its greatest ambassadors.

The charismatic and likeable German had been respected by fellow competitors and fans alike and his presence has been sorely missed by all. Klaus had been fully aware of the danger that road racing offered but believed that it was the risks that made it such a challenge and his 'raison d'etre'. In an era of Grand Prix prima donnas who never mix and hide away in their motor homes Klaus Klein was the epitome of a pure road racer by mixing with the fans and living life to the full, on and off the track.

44

SOLO LADIES AT THE T.T.

History was made in the 1954 Sidecar T.T. when the West German Frau Inge Stoll-Laforge became the first female to compete in the T.T. Races. She was the passenger to the French driver Jacques Drion and helped him into fifth place, in the race held on the Clypse Course. An anomaly, in the regulations of the day, allowed her to take part. The regulations stated : "Drivers should be male, aged between 18 and 55 years old", but the regulations for passengers stated: "passengers should be aged between 18 and 55 years old", there was no mention of their gender.

The role of the female competitor was restricted, to the not inconsiderable skill, of being a sidecar passenger until the regulations were changed for the inaugural 50cc T.T. in 1962. This was a surprising move by the F.I.M. considering the loss of the Swiss sidecar passenger Marie Lambert the previous year. Marie was the passenger for husband Claude, in the 1961 Sidecar T.T., when they crashed between Creg-ny-Baa and Brandish Corner with Marie suffering fatal injuries. Claude

Beryl Swain at the start of her historic ride in the 1962 50cc T.T.

returned to race on the Island the following year and has participated, in recent years, in the Classic Parade Lap held in T.T. week.

The challenge to race solos over the Mountain Course was taken up

101.03 mph – 1957
Senior
**Bob McIntyre
(Gilera)
First 100mph Lap.**

45

M

Memorials.

Many riders have, of course, given their lives to the sport that they loved. Memorials to these men are scattered around the course . . . some include . . . Karl Gall (Plaque in the Garden Wall opposite the Raven Inn), Dave Featherstone (Plaque on the Marshall's Hut at Alpine Cottage), Jimmy Guthrie (stone obelisk on the Mountain ascent), Les Graham Memorial (between the Verandah and Bungalow), Manfred Stengl (Marshall's hut at Keppel Gate) and then, of course, there is the Hailwood Centre at the rear of the Grandstand.

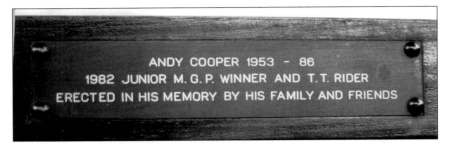

The Andy Cooper Memorial. *Courtesy Mike Hammonds*

Seat located at the Grandstand *Courtesy Mike Hammonds*

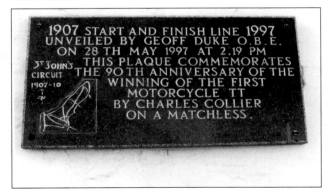

Plaque to commemorate the 1907 Start - Finish Line.
Courtesy Mike Hammonds

The Mike Hailwood Centre at the Grandstand
Courtesy Mike Hammonds

by Mrs. Beryl Swain, who entered her 50cc Itom in the 'Tiddlers Race'. This entry did not go unnoticed by the media, who gave her nearly as much attention as they did Mike Hailwood!! She finished twenty second of the twenty five finishers, in a time of 1 hour 33 minutes and 48 seconds, an average speed of 48.33 mph for the two laps.

Despite Beryl's courageous and safe ride, the F.I.M. Congress held in Brussels in the autumn of 1962 deemed: "That women competing in

Liz Skinner taking a pit stop during the 1988 Production 'D' T.T. held on Friday evening of practice week.

Courtesy Eric Whitehead

solo races could lead to 'bad publicity' for motorcycle sport if they were injured or worse", and thus they were barred from competing in international races. This did not, however, include women as sidecar passengers. The F.I.M. delegates represented thirty one countries but none spoke in favour of women competing in international solo races, although they could still compete on a national level. This international bar was not lifted until the mid 1970's.

The rules for the Manx Grand Prix precluded women from participating, but this ruling was challenged by Andrea Williams in 1972. Andrea, who was the sister of T.T. star Peter Williams and later married Tom Herron, had tried to

enter her 250cc Yamaha in the Lightweight M.G.P., but had been turned down under the "no female" rule. The Manx Motorcycle Club defended their position on the grounds that "The rules were the rules" and could not be changed. This would not be the last time they would try to defend their position.

Local government officer Phil Hodgkiss competed in the 1968 and 1977 M.G.P.s, failing to finish in both. He was given an entry for the 1978 Manx but was not allowed to ride. The M.G.P.'s committee suspicions had been raised by his appearance that was 'more shapely' than usual. They thought that a woman was trying to race on Hodgkiss's license. At the riders' briefing Hodgkiss admitted that he had undergone hormone treatment to enhance his figure and said : "I have adopted the lifestyle of a woman, it is a state of mind rather than a physical situation. Medically I am still a man and therefore they should let me race."

The 1978 T.T. programme was notable for the inclusion of one "S.M.B. Hailwood" and that of

**74.07 mph – 1958
Walter Schneider
(B.M.W.)
Fastest Lap Sidecar
Clypse Course**

Liz Skinner in the pit lane after averaging 84.87 mph on her TZR 250cc Yamaha in finishing 29th in the 1988 Production 'D' T.T.

Courtesy Eric Whitehead

Hilary Musson, the second female to be accepted to race solos at the T.T. Hailwood's comeback dominated the media's attention but Hilary raised more than the odd eyebrow. Fresh from coming third in the Avon 250cc Production Championship in 1977, she had gained the necessary

points in the early part of 1978 to obtain an international licence and thus qualify for entry into the T.T. As soon as it was announced that her entry had been accepted the media spotlight fell upon her. The ghouls from the press telephoned Hilary at work with the hope of extracting some garish and sensational stories. The media were out of luck, she felt that the fact that she was a woman competing in a dangerous, normally male dominated, event was incidental. This stance provoked a reaction from some media quarters who accused her of shunning publicity, she did, however, do an interview for the BBC's "Tonight" programme. History was created on the morning of Friday 9th June 1978, when Hilary set off at number 93 in the combined T.T. Formula 2 and 3 Race, because ten seconds earlier, her husband, John started. They became the first married couple to compete against each other in a solo race at the T.T. John finished fourteenth and Hilary was fifteenth, in the Formula 3 Race, in a time of 2 hours 1 minute and 5.8 seconds an average speed of 74.77 mph. Hilary competed in every T.T. up until and including 1985 but although generally reliable she always finished near the back of the field. She was refused an entry for the 1986 250cc Production T.T. because there were too many entrants. She appealed against the decision and the A.C.U. said: "taking into account her previous practice and race times, it was felt that she needed to gain more experience on race circuits at an international level before they could consider a further application." Hilary responded to this by saying "I know that I am a lot slower than some but I believed I was capable of reaching the qualifying time. I am

N

Nisbet Shield.

Named in memory of J. R. Nisbet, a former Chairman of the ACU, the Shield used to be awarded to "the competitor who exhibited such pluck, endurance or capacity to triumph over difficulties as to warrant some special prize". It was awarded on six occasions before being discontinued after the 1933 meeting. One recipient was G. W. Jones (New Hudson) who, following a crash at Sulby Bridge in the 1921 Junior T.T., was pitched into a stream. He scrambled out, straightened his machine, continued and finished 38th.

not dangerous, I have never fallen off on the T.T. Course and have never caused anyone to crash." That, unfortunately, brought an end to Hilary's T.T. racing career that amassed eight finishers awards. Hilary's last ride on the T.T. Course was whilst she was practicing for the Classic Lightweight Manx Grand Prix in 1989, unfortunately her

Kate Parkinson preparing for the start of the delayed 1998 Lightweight T.T.

Courtesy Albert Cooper, The Mirror

250cc Suzuki was not quick enough to qualify for the race.

The Musson family created history in 1998 when daughter Gail competed in the inaugural 125cc Newcomers Manx Grand Prix, becoming the first mother, father and daughter to compete in solo races over the Mountain Circuit.

The number of woman solo competitors was doubled for the 1984 T.T. with the arrival of the West German Margret Lingen. She was an engineering technician who designed and made furniture and had come fifth in the German Formula 2 Championship in 1983. She rode with a specially adapted bike, having lost three fingers on her left hand in an industrial accident.

The fastest lady ever over the Mountain Course . . . Sandra Barnett.

Courtesy Eric Whitehead

The front brake and clutch levers were both on the right hand handlebar. She entered both the Formula One and Formula Two

80.22 mph – 1959
250cc
Tarquino Provini (MV Agusta) Fastest Lap Clypse Course

T.T.s, riding Ducatis. She finished practice by being the fastest ever woman around the Island on a solo machine with a lap of 92.88 mph on her 750cc Ducati. Her ambition was to learn the course and get two finishers awards with the hope of returning the following year to win a replica. Margret's first race on the Mountain Course is probably one that she would wish to forget, she fell off at Quarter Bridge on the first lap in front of a huge crowd of spectators, journalists and photographers. The following day's tabloids all had pictures of her misdemeanor and her story. Of the crash she said: "As I came down the hill towards the Quarter Bridge the front wheel wobbled and the bike slid from underneath me. I am determined the Formula Two Race will be different and I will show that women can compete with men on the T.T. Course." In recognition of her endeavours she was presented with the Joey Dunlop video 'V for Victory' by the Isle of Man Tourist Board. She said "The video is great, Joey will be a good instructor. I like corners and the T.T. is full of them, I want to conquer the course and my problem is I don't know the corners and the video will help me to remember". In the Formula Two Race she finished twenty eighth averaging 93.29 mph. Margret entered the 1985 and 1986 T.T.'s but didn't race in either. In 1985, her sponsor refused to give her permission to take his machines to the Island, and in 1986, she crashed at the Nurburgring, seriously damaging her hand.

The campaign to allow women to ride in the Manx Grand Prix was gathering pace. Liz Skinner, who, in 1987, was the first lady solo rider to compete in the Southern 100, applied to race in the Lightweight Newcomers Manx Grand Prix . Her entry, and that of Hilary Musson to ride in the Senior Classic, were turned down by the Manx Motorcycle Club. Liz was so incensed that she threatened to take her case to the European Court of Human Rights. She was the current lap record holder at Bridlington, had won races there and at Carnaby and Elvington. The Manx Motorcycle Club had accepted entries from male riders who she had consistently beaten on the U.K. short circuits, and she felt that this was wrong. Bill Bennett, secretary of the Manx, said that Liz Skinner's

Sandra Barnett at Quarter Bridge on the first lap of the 1977 Production T.T Sanyo Honda CBR 900 Fireblade (25th at 109.49 mph.)

Courtesy Peter Wilcock

application had arrived after the regulations were fixed and it was too late to alter them. The regulations stated that riders must be male and over eighteen years of age, and these had been in place since 1923. In August of 1987, a group calling themselves 'Team She Daytona', petitioned Number Ten Downing Street. The leaders of the team, Denise Old, Peta Wootton and Angela Ridealgh were trying to persuade Margaret Thatcher, the Prime Minister, to support their plea

for women to compete in the M.G.P. It would be another two years before their wish would come true.

Undeterred, Liz Skinner decided to enter the 250cc Production T.T. in 1988. Her entry wasn't plain sailing, she was told that she would need the maximum fifteen international points to secure a ride, knowing full well that other riders were given a 'one day' licence to ride. After qualifying her 250cc TZR Yamaha for the race she said : "It is crazy that they will allow me to race against some of the best riders in the world but ban me from riding against men of a similar standard to myself in the M.G.P." Practice wasn't without its setbacks as Liz crashed twice, without injury, at Quarter Bridge and at the Nook. The race went rather better, she finished twenty-ninth with a race average of 84.87

mph. and was a member of the winning club team, Auto 66, along with Derek Chatterton and Neil Tuxworth. She said at the finish : "I had tears in my eyes as I came down from the Creg on the last lap, I am so pleased to get to the finish."

The pressure on the Manx Motorcycle Club to allow woman to race carried on gaining momentum and in January 1989 Club Chairman Geoff Karran made the following announcement : "In the interests of equality we will accept women entries to the M.G.P. In the past we have been concerned about the possibility of adverse publicity if there was an accident and serious injury involving a female competitor." A new era was about to dawn with an influx of women racing in the M.G.P. and by 1997 fifteen women had competed in the event,

four of whom also rode in the T.T.

The new era was lead by Kate Parkinson who became the first lady to average over 100 mph, which she unofficially achieved in practice for the 1992 Lightweight M.G.P. but could not make it official in the race due to the poor weather conditions. She didn't have long to wait for she entered the 1993 T.T. and lapped at 104.91 mph on her 250cc TZ Yamaha in the Junior with a race average of 102.02 mph. This was a far cry from her first visit to the Manx just two years previous, she had gained a silver replica in the Junior Newcomers Race but had crashed heavily at Sarah's Cottage in the Lightweight Race. She was knocked unconscious and air-lifted to hospital, fortunately without any lasting injury. Kate continued her progress and in the 1997 Lightweight T.T. she had a fastest lap

101.05 mph – 1960
Senior
Derek Minter (Norton)
First 100mph Lap
Single cylinder machine

of 110.16 mph on her 250cc TZ-G Yamaha, gaining a bronze replica with a race average of 108.13 mph in finishing sixteenth.

As Kate Parkinson concentrated on the smaller classes, it was left to Sandra Barnett to pick up the 750cc mantle. Sandra and her team brought a new look to women's racing with a totally professional approach. Image and attention to detail brought the team exposure and sponsorship. This, however, would not have been the case if it had not also been for the not inconsiderable talent of the rider. Sandra came fifth, on a 600cc Honda, in the 1993 Junior Newcomers M.G.P. with a race average of 104.54 mph and a fastest lap of 106.21 mph. She also raced in the Senior M.G.P., finishing fifteenth and winning a silver replica. Sandra's race average was 106.32 mph and her final lap was an amazing 108.21 mph. This made her the fastest lady ever to race around the T.T. Circuit. Sandra showed her versatility by racing in all solo classes at the T.T. from 250cc upwards, she also rode a Greeves in the Classic Manx. She holds the female lap record at the T.T. in all classes that she competes in and is the only female rider to win a silver replica. This was achieved in 1996 when she came twelfth in the Junior. Sandra, along with sponsor George Pilkington, created an all women's racing team in 1996 and sent a team to the Manx Grand Prix which included Maria Costello and Bridget McManus.

The only foreign female solo competitor, other than Margret

O

Ossa.

This Spanish company was started in 1940 by ex-road racer and industrialist Manuel Giro, concentrating on the smaller capacity classes. The marque won the 1965 Barcelona 24 Hour Race and achieved its only T.T. victory in 1968. Trevor Burgess won the 250cc Production Class with a start-to-finish victory . . . But the most notable Ossa rider was flamboyant Spaniard Santiago Herrero. After finishing third in the 1969 Lightweight class behind Kel Carruthers (Benelli) and Frank Perris (Suzuki), Herrero was tipped for possible victory the following year. In the race, however, he never featured in the top three, but on the final lap he collided with Cheshire rider Stanley Woods and received fatal injuries. The works Ossa machines were never seen on the road racing scene again.

The fated Santiago Herrero.

P

Practicing.

This takes place during the five days prior to the F1 and Sidecar Races; there are now fewer sessions than in earlier years with the roads being closed for only three early morning sessions . . . road closure was not always the order of the day. In 1927 Archie Birkin was thrown into a wall and killed when trying to avoid a fish van making early morning deliveries in the Kirk Michael area. The bend was re-named in memory of Birkin and the roads were closed for practice from 1928.

Q

Quadrant.

This little-raced machine actually made five starts. A retirement on the St. John's course in 1910 with W. Pollard aboard in his only T.T. race, in 1913 and 1914 the marque had 29th, 35th and 49th positions, together with one retirement in the Senior race.

Lingen, to tackle the Mountain Course is Italian Francesca Giordano. She first rode in 1992 but did not complete a practice lap due to mechanical problems with her Aprillia. She returned the following year and was the final finisher in the Supersport 400 Race. Her striking appearance has created a lot of media attention and many of the national daily's have done articles on her over the last few years. It is unfortunate that her T.T. results have not been more successful to maximise the publicity.

The Ninetieth Anniversary of the T.T. was celebrated in 1997, and this coincided with the first woman to enter the Sidecar T.T. as a driver. Wendy Davis, from Bristol, and passenger Martyn Roberts entered their Honda 600cc machine. They qualified sixty-second with a fastest lap of 87.38 mph. set during the Thursday afternoon practice session. They finished forty-second in Sidecar Race 'A' with a race average of 88.11 mph. and a fastest lap of 88.64 mph. Wendy went even faster in Sidecar Race 'B', with a race average of 90.32 mph. and a fastest lap of 90.97 mph. She finished forty-first and collected her second finishers award of the week.

The perils and dangers of riding the Mountain Course are there for all to see and most of the women competitors have taken a tumble, fortunately, most without injury. The Manx Motorcycle Club's greatest fear occurred in practice for the 1997 Manx Grand Prix. Local rider, Pamela Cannell, was fatally injured when she crashed her 250cc

Yamaha on the Verandah. Pamela had competed in the previous year's M.G.P. when she finished fifth in the Newcomers Lightweight Race.

Sandra Barnett stands out as the fastest ever women T.T. rider, however the most successful are sidecar passengers. The first lady to stand on the rostrum was Rose Arnold (now Mrs. Roy Hanks), who came second in the 1968 750cc Sidecar T.T. as passenger to future brother-in-law Norman Hanks. The most successful lady of all time was Julia Bingham who came runner-up on three occasions (1982/83/84) and third in 1985. She was passenger to husband Dennis and they were one of the greatest sidecar teams not to win a T.T.

The T.T and Manx Grand Prix are all the better for having women competing on equal terms with their male counterparts. Hopefully it will not be too long into the distant future that we will see a woman climbing the rostrum stairs to receive her laurels.

90.70 mph – 1962
Max Deubel
(B.M.W.)
First 90 mph Lap
Sidecar

KIWI INVASION

From the onset of racing on the T.T. Mountain Circuit riders from New Zealand have come to the Isle of Man. The first to make the journey was W. Johnson in 1911 who finished ninth in the Junior and fourteenth in the Senior on Humber machines. It wasn't until the 1950's that a Kiwi won a T.T. race, and that honour went to Rod Coleman in 1954, who won the Junior on a 350cc A.J.S. Further victories followed for Hugh Anderson, Graeme Crosby, Dennis Ireland and the late Robert Holden.

Although many riders have made the long trip to the Island most have done it under their own steam with little or no help from the sport's governing bodies. Ever spiraling costs throughout the 1980s reduced the number of Kiwis prepared to travel the distance to a trickle. By the early 1990s the Manx authorities recognized that the Island was not maximising its potential in terms of attracting Antipodeans to the T.T. It was felt that riders from New Zealand were ideally suited to racing on the Mountain Course, having been brought up on the street circuits at home. To this end the Isle

of Man Tourist Board contacted the New Zealand A.C.U. in 1993 to set up a scholarship, whereby a young Kiwi would be funded, jointly, by the two bodies to race at the T.T. The head of the New Zealand A.C.U., John Shand, thought it was an excellent idea and the wheels were set in motion to choose an up and coming rider to race in the 1994 T.T. Shand had visited the Island for

Maudes Trophy Team Captain Robert Holden seen at Parliament Square during the 1992 Formula One T.T.
Courtesy Eric Whitehead

the first time in 1993 with the John Britten Racing Team. New Zealander Shaun Harris had ridden the Britten 1000cc V Twin in the Senior T.T.

T.T. Clerk of the Course Jack Wood travelled to New Zealand in late March of 1994 to meet with John Shand and choose the lucky rider. The current Kiwi 250cc Champion John Hepburn, 28, was granted the scholarship and he would ride a Ron Grant prepared Honda CBR 600 with backing from Michelin Tyres. Jack Wood found that John Shand was a man of action and not just words, for twenty-six riders had applied for the scholarship. John Shand had set up a team of sixteen riders, including Hepburn, to race in the Isle of Man in June. An overjoyed Jack Wood left New Zealand with the job of trying to secure some extra sponsorship for this team.

The T.T. entries closed with a total of eighteen riders coming from New Zealand. This included a ten man team to contest for the Maudes Trophy, in the Supersport 600 Race; plus scholarship winner John Hepburn, G.P. regular Andrew Stroud and T.T. stalwarts Robert Holden, Shaun Harris and Glen Williams. Added to these were newcomers Loren Poole, Michael Willemson and Stephen Briggs.

The Maudes Trophy

John Shand was a bike importer and by coincidence had the same Japanese contact as A.C.U. Chairman Bill Smith. It was Smith who put Shand in contact with Mitsui Yamaha and they suggested the Maudes Trophy attempt. The

Maudes Trophy, last awarded in 1984 to Heron Suzuki, is presented by the A.C.U. for outstanding achievements of reliability for production based machines. The New Zealanders would all have to finish the 150 mile Supersport 600 Race to qualify. They were to race FZR600R Yamahas; these were brand new machines that had to be unpacked and assembled in front of A.C.U. technical committee man Ernie Woods. Woods had previously been to the Mitsui Yamaha headquarters and randomly selected ten bikes from stock. The team, managed by ex-T.T. rider Noel McCutcheon, had new Arai helmets, Metzeler tyres and received further assistance from Silkolene Oil, Mobil petrol, Nippon Denso plugs and Ferodo brakes. Once on the Island,

Grand Prix competitor Andrew Stroud, knee down, flying across the Mountain in the 1994 Supersport 600 T.T. finishing twenty-sixth and gaining a bronze replica.
Courtesy Eric Whitehead

90.13 mph – 1962
Luigi Taveri
(Honda)
First 90 mph Lap
125cc T.T.

the team were given celebrity status, and the Mayor gave them a civic reception at Douglas Town Hall.

The team certainly had its work cut out in preparing the bikes and the riders for practice. The bikes were always under the careful eye of Ernie Woods to make sure that there was no infringement of the Maudes Trophy Rules. Practice started well, and by Wednesday it was clear that they had a real star in Jason McEwan. McEwan had lapped at 111.35 mph on Tuesday evening, with all but two of the team averaging over 100 mph. Hugh Reynolds had fallen off at Laurel Bank, without injury. Spirits in the camp were high but the team were less than twenty-four hours away from their lowest ebb. McEwan increased his speed on Wednesday evening to 113.10 mph to qualify tenth for the race. Thursday afternoon practice saw teamster Doug Bell fall off at Brandywell, without injury, but Britten rider, Mark Farmer, was fatally injured when he had crashed at the Black Dub. The Britten Team were sharing the same facilities as the Maudes Team and Farmer had been a popular figure, giving help and advice. His demise had thrown a dark vale over the 'happy go lucky' Kiwis. Robert Holden withdrew his Britten from the Formula One Race, but Nick Jefferies decided to race his. Holden said "I have not been happy with the bike all week, and I told John Britten, before Mark's accident, that I would not ride it in the race". Jason McEwan took the Britten out for practice on Friday

The Maudes Trophy Team with Team Manager Noel McCutcheon.
Courtesy Peter Wilcock

evening, but could only lap at 87.84 mph in the wet. This was not considered sufficient to qualify for the race.

Practice week concluded with every member of the team averaging over 100 mph. The fastest was McEwan who qualified tenth fastest at 113.10 mph. and slowest was Doug Bell at 101.08 mph. Scholarship winner, John Hepburn, lapped at 108.668 mph on Thursday afternoon to qualify thirty-second, G.P. runner Andrew Stroud qualified twenty-seventh at 110.61 mph and Chris Haldane was twenty-fifth at 110.70 mph. Haldane's father had ridden the T.T. in the late 1960's and early 1970's. Loren Poole, who was not a member of the Maudes Team, qualified fifteenth. He lapped at

112.03 mph. during the Thursday afternoon practice session. John Shand was delighted with how well all the Kiwi riders had taken to the Mountain Course.

The Winning Team

The team's nerve was tested to the full as race day approached. The weather forecast was not promising with wind and rain expected, in fact conditions on race day were so poor that racing was postponed until the following day. The race finally got

Ill-fated Mark Farmer, aboard the 160 bhp. C.R.S. 1000cc Britten, on his way to a lap of 118.21 mph. during practice for the 1994 Formula One T.T. before being tragically killed at the Black Dub the following day.

Courtesy Eric Whitehead

under way on Tuesday 7th June with much improved weather conditions. To qualify for the Trophy all ten riders had to finish the race, on their standard road going machines, and then they would have to wait to see if the A.C.U. Panel felt it was meritorious enough to be awarded the Trophy. The first lap of the race was completed successfully. Team leader Robert Holden lead the way in eleventh place with a lap of 112.75 mph, followed by McEwan in twentieth at 109.82 mph, Blair Degerholm brought up the rear in seventy-sixth place at 89.70 mph. Degerholm improved from his poor start on the second lap to seventieth position with a lap of 105.09 mph, Holden was in twelfth position with McEwan sixteenth and Haldane thirtieth. They all successfully negotiated their pit stops and all ten were still running at the start of the last lap. The whole Island was willing the team to finish, and one by one they crossed the line at the end. First to finish was Holden in a fantastic ninth place, followed by McEwan in thirteenth, Haldane thirtieth, Russell Josiah forty-fourth,

100.90 mph – 1962
Gary Hocking
(MV Agusta)
First 100 mph Lap
Junior T.T.

Shaun Harris aboard the V Twin 1000cc Britten on its debut appearance in 1993.

Courtesy Eric Whitehead

Nathan Spargo forty-sixth, Anthony Young fiftieth, Paul Williams fifty-third, Hugh Reynolds fifty-fifth, Blair Degerholm sixty-first and finally Douglas Bell in sixty-second position. To add to this success, Loren Poole finished fifteenth, Andrew Stroud twenty-sixth, John Hepburn twenty-eighth, Michael Willemson fortieth and finally Stephen Briggs was forty-fifth. It was a very proud and delighted John Shand who announced that all fifteen Kiwi starters had finished the race, which, of course, included the Maudes Trophy Team. The A.C.U. panel met on July 6th 1994 and awarded the Kiwi and Yamaha team

the Maudes Trophy for performance and reliability. The ten man team averaged 104.78 mph for the four lap race and each bike averaged 1278 miles for practicing and racing. Petrol was consumed at an average of 47.98 miles per gallon.

The Shand Influence

In the years that followed only three riders of the Maudes Team failed to return to the Island, they were Jason McEwan, Russell Josiah and Anthony Young. It was a great shame that McEwan didn't return to fulfill his potential but the T.T. is that

The Yamaha FZR 600Rs to be ridden in the Maudes Trophy attempt, complete with revised race numbers.

Courtesy Mike Hammonds

81.10 mph – 1964
Hugh Anderson
(Suzuki)
First 80 m.p.h. Lap
50cc T.T.

Nick Jefferies persisted with the Britten, but retired on the second lap of both the Formula One and the Senior T.T.s in 1994.
Courtesy Mike Hammonds

(Left)
The impressive Jason McEwan at the Bungalow on his way to thirteenth place in the 1994 Supersport 600cc T.T.
Courtesy Eric Whitehead

(Below left)
Loren Poole on his way to winning a silver replica, with an excellent fifteenth place and a race average of 110.79 mph. in the Supersport 600 T.T.
Courtesy Eric Whitehead

much healthier for the return of his compatriots. John Shand was certainly bitten by the bug and continued to bring new riders to the event. In the winter of 1996 he moved to Sweden and started to spread the T.T. message. He entered a twelve man team for the 1997 races which included eight New Zealanders and four Swedes. The debt the T.T. owes John Shand can be seen by counting the number of newcomers that he has brought to the event, a total of twenty-eight. The majority of whom have returned

**100.01 mph – 1965
Phil Read
(Yamaha)
First 100 mph Lap
250cc T.T.**

to race in subsequent years. It is also interesting to note that the original winner of the New Zealand scholarship, John Hepburn, has returned every year since.

(Right)
Maudes Trophy Team member Anthony Young at Quarter Bridge in the 1994 Supersport 600cc T.T.

Courtesy Mike Hammonds

(Below)
Maudes Trophy Team member Blair Degerholm at Quarter Bridge in the 1994 Supersport 600cc T.T.

Courtesy Mike Hammonds

Maudes Trophy Team member
Hugh Reynolds at Quarter Bridge
in the 1994 Supersport 600cc T.T.

Courtesy Mike Hammonds

Nathan Spargo, who has now
become a T.T. regular with the
John Shand Racing Team.

Courtesy Mike Hammonds

85.66 mph – 1966
Ralph Bryans
(Honda)
Fastest Lap by a
50cc machine

ORIGIN

The T.T. Races prides itself on being a truly international event . . . but from where have the riders come to compete in the world's greatest road races? Listed are the first to arrive from the different countries and the year in which they came . . .

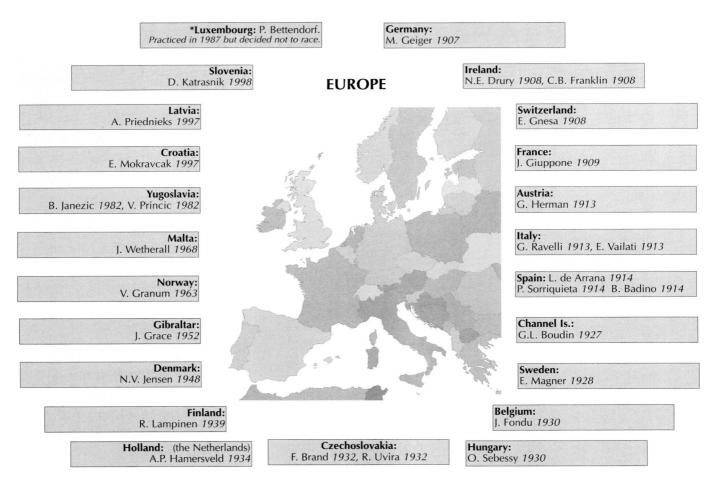

*Luxembourg: P. Bettendorf. *Practiced in 1987 but decided not to race.*

Germany: M. Geiger *1907*

Slovenia: D. Katrasnik *1998*

EUROPE

Ireland: N.E. Drury *1908*, C.B. Franklin *1908*

Latvia: A. Priednieks *1997*

Switzerland: E. Gnesa *1908*

Croatia: E. Mokravcak *1997*

France: J. Giuppone *1909*

Yugoslavia: B. Janezic *1982*, V. Princic *1982*

Austria: G. Herman *1913*

Malta: J. Wetherall *1968*

Italy: G. Ravelli *1913*, E. Vailati *1913*

Norway: V. Granum *1963*

Spain: L. de Arrana *1914* P. Sorriquieta *1914* B. Badino *1914*

Gibraltar: J. Grace *1952*

Channel Is.: G.L. Boudin *1927*

Denmark: N.V. Jensen *1948*

Sweden: E. Magner *1928*

Finland: R. Lampinen *1939*

Belgium: J. Fondu *1930*

Holland: (the Netherlands) A.P. Hamersveld *1934*

Czechoslovakia: F. Brand *1932*, R. Uvira *1932*

Hungary: O. Sebessy *1930*

OF RIDERS

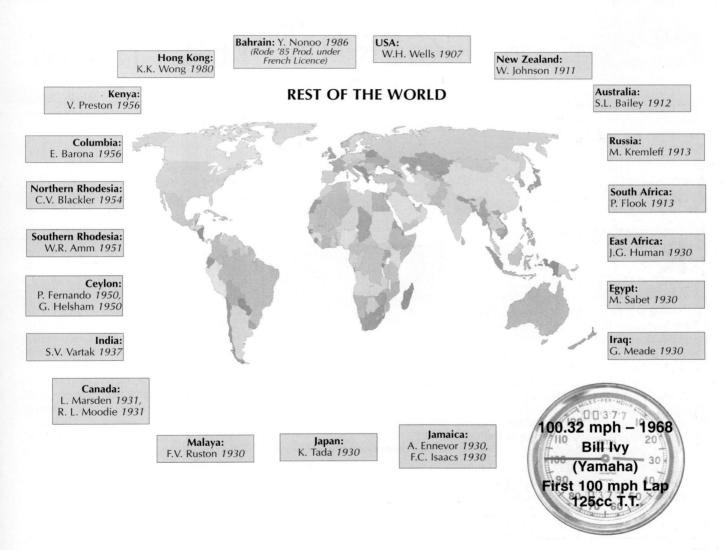

REST OF THE WORLD

Bahrain: Y. Nonoo *1986*
(Rode '85 Prod. under French Licence)

Hong Kong:
K.K. Wong *1980*

USA:
W.H. Wells *1907*

New Zealand:
W. Johnson *1911*

Kenya:
V. Preston *1956*

Australia:
S.L. Bailey *1912*

Columbia:
E. Barona *1956*

Russia:
M. Kremleff *1913*

Northern Rhodesia:
C.V. Blackler *1954*

South Africa:
P. Flook *1913*

Southern Rhodesia:
W.R. Amm *1951*

East Africa:
J.G. Human *1930*

Ceylon:
P. Fernando *1950,*
G. Helsham *1950*

Egypt:
M. Sabet *1930*

India:
S.V. Vartak *1937*

Iraq:
G. Meade *1930*

Canada:
L. Marsden *1931,*
R. L. Moodie *1931*

Malaya:
F.V. Ruston *1930*

Japan:
K. Tada *1930*

Jamaica:
A. Ennevor *1930,*
F.C. Isaacs *1930*

**100.32 mph – 1968
Bill Ivy
(Yamaha)
First 100 mph Lap
125cc T.T.**

ON APPEAL –
A TIGER IN THE TANK

Scheidegger and Robinson leaving Ramsey during their controversial victory.

Fifty-six crews lined up on August Bank Holiday Sunday for the historic 1966 Sidecar T.T. The meeting had been postponed due to the Seaman's Strike and so, in order to cram the Manx Grand Prix and the T.T. into a hectic four week period, T.T. racing took place on a Sunday for the first time.

The race was dominated by BMW machinery - Germans Max Deubel and Emil Horner, victors the previous year, led for their first two circuits from Swiss driver Fritz Scheidegger with John Robinson from Purley in the chair. A useful 15 second lead disappeared at Union Mills on lap three as Deubel's machine seized, pouring out oil as he tried to coax it to restart. Restart it did, but Scheidegger took the initiative, winning by one of the narrowest of margins - 4/5ths of a second - despite his five speed gearbox bursting as he came out of Governor's Bridge dip with just a few hundred yards to the finish. . . but . . .

There was even greater drama to come . . . The Swiss ace was disqualified! A protest had been made that he had used Esso fuel and not Shell as stated on his 'Declaration' submitted at the weigh-in. Deubel was announced as the winner and received his trophy amidst rowdy scenes at that evening's Presentation. Scheidegger appealed to the F.I.M. jury but was turned down; only after a long, drawn out wait of nearly three months did he successfully appeal to the R.A.C. Stewards. He was re-instated as the winner, awarded the prize money, and gained vital World Champion-

---

R

Tommy Robb.

Everyone's favourite of the day, Tommy Robb from Belfast, - now a motorcycle dealer in Warrington, raced for 22 years. First on the rough and then on the roads. A versatile racer, he rode such a variety of machinery - N.S.U., Norton, G.M.S., Ducati, Matchless, A.J.S., Bultaco, Honda, Yamaha, Suzuki and Seeley. He was a runner-up in the 350 and 3rd in the 125 classes of the 1962 World Championships, but it was his long awaited T.T. victory in the 1973 125cc Race, after 15 years, for which he will be best remembered.

Tommy Robb leads the Suzuki charge of Anderson, Degner and Ansheidt around Quarter Bridge in the '66 50cc T.T..
Courtesy FoTTofinders Archive Research System

S

Scouts.

Earliest records show Scout involvement in the races since 1909. In the early days Semaphore Scouts were placed around the whole T.T. course, about 300 yards apart. Their duty was to watch for and endeavour to prevent accidents (as the Flag Marshals do today), pass messages to the Marshals, call for medical assistance or, if able, render first aid and assist in keeping the course clear. Today they work on the scoreboards, operating the clocks and pulling the tear-offs etc. and, of course, carrying the flags of the competing nations on the starting grid.

Scouts spruce up Geoff Davidson's winning 250cc Levis during a 1922 Pit Stop. *Courtesy FoTTofinders Archive Research System*

ship points. He was indeed the '66 World Champion, as he was in '65, but it was not to be three in a row as he was tragically killed in a Mallory Park Easter Sunday accident on his first 1967 appearance in England. John Robinson survived but retired from the sport.

Deubel and Horner had retired at the end of the '66 season having won three T.T.s and four World Championships. Deubel then ran the family hotel in the village of Muhlenhau, near Cologne, and later served the sport as an F.I.M. official.

T

Kenzo Tada.

Japanese riders really hit the T.T. scene in the late '50s and early '60s, but the first rider from the land of the Rising Sun to compete was Kenzo Tada in the Junior T.T. of 1930. Problems during practice meant he was off his Velocette machine at least twice - at Ballacraine and The Nook, above Governor's Bridge. However, he was fit to race, finishing 15th, 21 minutes behind winner H.G. Tyrell-Smith.

100.37 mph – 1969 Malcolm Uphill (Triumph) First 100 mph Lap Production T.T.

U

Carlo Ubbiali

Carlo Ubbiali.

An Italian mechanic from Bergamo had a remarkable T.T. record. He first rode in 1951, finishing second in the 125cc class on his Mondial behind Cromie McCandless. Same again the following year, but this time he followed Cecil Sandford home. The remainder of his T.T. career was aboard 125cc and 250cc MV Agusta machinery . . . his final tally from 15 starts was five victories, including the double in 1956, seven second places, one fifth and only two retirements. Ubbiali won 9 World Championships, doubling up in 1959 and 1960, the year he retired.

V

Terry Vinicombe.

Prior to 1968 the Sidecar class was for 500cc capacity machines, but in this year a 750 class was run concurrently with these GP combinations. After Chris Vincent retired, Terry Vinicombe brought his Kirby B.S.A. home in first place at 85.85 mph. This was the last time B.S.A. machinery was victorious at the T.T.; the outfit ridden so ably by Vinicombe and John Flaxman is on display at the British Motorcycle Museum in Birmingham. The Terry Vinicombe Trophy is

Terry Vinicombe and John Flaxman aboard their winning BSA.

awarded each year for the best performance in either Sidecar Race by a driver and passenger ordinarily resident in the British Isles driving a machine of British manufacture.

HONDA - THE GOLDEN YEARS

Ian Lougher set another landmark for the Honda Motor Corporation when he won the Lightweight T.T. at the Ninetieth Anniversary of the races in 1997. This victory, fittingly, was the ninetieth to be achieved on a Honda since they first rode on the Isle of Man in 1959. This is the story of how Honda first came into road racing and how they dominated the T.T. before they withdrew from the racing scene at the end of 1967, for the period 1959 until 1967 were the Honda Golden Years.

Soichiro Honda, who headed the company, had a vision of making The Honda Motor Corporation the world leader in the production and selling of motorcycles. To achieve this ambition he needed to produce quality motorcycles that could be sold world-wide. In order to get the necessary recognition he believed that he would need to create a race team that would travel to Europe and win the World Championship Classic Races. With this thought firmly in mind he travelled to Europe in 1954 to survey the competition and make plans for the future. Soichiro went to the Isle of Man and witnessed the world famous T.T.

The beginning of an era, Honda's Twin cylinder RC 142 125cc machine pictured at the 1959 T.T.

Races and it was while he was there that he convinced himself that for Honda to really make its mark it would have to win a T.T. He returned to Japan with many

107.27 mph – 1973
Peter Williams
(Norton)
Fastest Lap
F750

thoughts and as many bike parts that he could possibly carry. The German N.S.U. bikes had most impressed Soichiro with their slick design and speed and he would use these images to model the new Honda racing motorcycles. The intention was to return to Europe the following year with the newly designed Hondas, however development took longer than Soichiro had originally planned and it wouldn't be until 1959 that the Hondas would venture west.

T.T. Debut

Soichiro Honda was sufficiently happy with the development of the new 125cc Honda that they would compete in the 1959 Isle of Man T.T. Races. They originally entered the production based Formula races but their entry was declined as these were for 350cc and 500cc capacity machines and the Honda was only 125cc. The Honda Team entry was accepted for the ten lap 107.9 mile 125cc race over the Clypse Course and consisted of five riders, four of whom were Japanese and the fifth an American, all newcomers to the T.T. The American, Billy Hunt, also acted as team leader and technical advisor.

The stylish design of the Honda four-stroke 125cc twins was unsurprisingly similar to the N.S.U. Rennmax machines so admired by Soichiro Honda from his original visit to Europe. The dhoc engines were shaft driven and had a bore and stroke of 44mm x 41mm which

produced 18.5 bhp. It was clear from practice that the Hondas lacked speed compared to their European counterparts but what they lacked in this area they made up for in reliability. The race brought great pride to the Japanese with Honda winning the prestigious Manufacturers Team Award, with four of the five Hondas finishing the race. Most successful was Naomi Taniguchi who finished sixth gaining a silver replica, followed by Giichi Suzuki, seventh and Teisuke Tanaka, eighth, both winning bronze replicas. The final finisher was Junzo Suzuki who came home eleventh; Bill Hunt had crashed on the second lap without injury but had been forced to retire.

This first foray into the racing

Naomi Taniguchi (10) sixth 1959 125cc T.T. and nineteenth 1960 125cc T.T.
Teisuke Tanaka (11) eighth 1959 125cc T.T. and ninth 1960 125cc T.T.
Kunimitsu Takahashi (8) fourth 1961 250cc T.T. and eighth 1963 125cc T.T.
Picture taken at the Honda Anniversary Parade in the Isle of Man in 1998.
Courtesy Albert Cooper, The Mirror

world had certainly whetted the appetite and Soichiro Honda was determined to return the following year with much improved machinery and a more experienced riding team in order to make a full assault on the 1960 World Championship. Honda's exploits at the T.T. had not gone unnoticed and their potential was recognised by the Australian Tom Phillis. Phillis wrote to Honda at the end of the 1959 season requesting to join the team and this was an offer Honda could not refuse. Phillis was a rising star and was just the rider and profile that Honda were looking for.

Development work back in Japan went unabated and the information gained from the Island was invaluable but incomplete. 1959 proved to be the last time the Clypse Course would be used with all races taking place on the Mountain Course from 1960. Honda produced two brand new bikes for the 1960 season, a 125cc twin and a 250cc four cylinder machine, both of which would find the rigours of the Mountain Course extremely demanding.

Lack of speed was again the issue in the 125cc T.T. with Hondas filling positions sixth to tenth inclusively. Taniguchi again coming sixth with Giichi Suzuki seventh, newcomer Sadao Shimazaki eighth, Tanaka ninth, Phillis tenth and Moto Kitano nineteenth. Australian Bob Brown took over Tanaka's machine for the 250cc T.T. and came a very encouraging fourth behind the M.V.'s of winner Hocking and Ubbialli, and third placed Morini rider, Provini. There was further delight for Honda with Kitano coming home fifth and Taniguchi once again sixth, Phillis and Giichi Suzuki both retired with mechanical

problems. Tragedy was to befall the team later that year when Bob Brown was killed whilst practising for the German Grand Prix at Solitude.

Fortune Shines

The events at the end of the 1960 season could not have been more fortuitous for the Honda team; M.V. Agusta withdrew from competing in the smaller World Championship classes to concentrate their efforts on Gary Hocking in the 350cc and 500cc events. Nine times World Champion Carlo Ubbiali, who had won the last three 125cc and last two 250cc World Championships, announced his retirement following the

Tom Phillis and his mechanic working on the Four cylinder Honda RC 161 250cc machine prior to the 1960 Lightweight T.T.

110.71 mph – 1976
Classic
**John Williams (Suzuki)
First 110 mph Lap**

withdrawal of his M.V. factory support. Ubbiali's retirement coincided with the defection of seven times World Champion John Surtees to car racing, depriving motorcycle racing of two of its greatest protagonists.

Honda were not slow to exploit this opportunity and increased their team for the 1961 season. Rhodesian Jim Redman had joined the team mid-way through the previous year after Tom Phillis had crashed and injured himself at the Dutch T.T. and these two were joined by the diminutive Swiss star Luigi Taveri, latterly of M.V. The rest of the team was made up of the Japanese riders, Taniguchi, Kitano, Shimazaki and Kunimitsu Takahashi; Mike Hailwood and Bob McIntrye were loaned bikes to give extra depth. This enlarged team coupled with major development work on both the 125cc and 250cc machines meant that Honda would be a world force in 1961.

At the T.T. Honda claimed the first five places in the 125cc and 250cc races with Mike Hailwood winning both classes. Luigi Taveri and Tom Phillis followed Hailwood home in

(Top right)
Tom Phillis at the bottom of Bray Hill in the 1960 Lightweight Race before mechanical problems forced him to retire.
(Right)
Behind the fairing , the 1960 Honda RC 161 Four Cylinder 250cc machine.

the 125cc and Phillis and Jim Redman were behind him in the 250cc race. Soichiro Honda's dream had been fulfilled within three years of competition, albeit with a non-Japanese rider. New lap and race records were set in both races with Taveri setting the new 125cc mark and Bob McIntrye the 250cc lap records with Hailwood taking the race records. Honda completed a highly successful T.T. by winning the Manufacturers Awards in both races. Mike Hailwood finished a record breaking week by becoming the first rider to win three T.T. races in a week when he won the Senior T.T. on a Norton after Hocking had retired his M.V., it could so easily have been four but for a broken gudgeon pin forcing him to retire in the Junior giving victory to Phil Read. The Senior Race saw Derek Minter just pipping Hailwood to become the first to lap the Mountain Course at over 100 mph. on a single cylinder machine and winning a £100 from Mike's father to boot !

Honda's T.T. success was mirrored in the World Championship with Phillis claiming the 125cc and Hailwood the 250cc titles. Soichiro Honda had now succeeded in putting the Honda name at the pinnacle of the motorcycling world and giving him a real platform to sell his production bikes from.

Triumph and Tragedy

The 1962 season saw Honda maintain their challenge in the 125cc and 250cc classes but

they also entered the inaugural 50cc World Championship and the 350cc event. To take on the might of the M.V. in the Junior Class Honda produced a 285cc four cylinder engine that had a bore and stroke of 49mm x 45mm which revved to 12,500 rpm. producing 50 bhp. Tommy Robb had signed for Honda in the close season and Mike Hailwood had secured a works contract with M.V. to contest the 350cc and 500cc World Championships.

The 125cc Ultra-Lightweight and 250cc Lightweight T.T.'s were a clean sweep for Honda with Taveri winning the former from Robb and Phillis and Derek Minter winning the latter from Redman and Phillis. Minter's 250cc win was a bittersweet victory for Honda

Bob Brown, at the bottom of Bray Hill, on his way to fourth place on the works Honda RC 161 250cc machine during the 1960 Lightweight T.T.

because he was privately entered and had beaten the established Honda stars. Bob McIntyre once

**100.59 mph – 1977
Dick Greasley
(Yamaha)
First 100mph Lap
Sidecar**

again set the fastest lap of the race but was one of seventeen retirements in a field of twenty-five starters and only eight finishers, one of whom (D. Guy) was classed as a fifth lap finisher.

The new 285cc four cylinder Honda made its debut in Wednesday's Junior T.T. with Tom Phillis starting first at number one with Franta Stastny on the Jawa alongside, Bob McIntyre rode the second Honda at number ten. At the end of the first lap Gary Hocking lead from team mate Hailwood and third placed Phillis with just a couple of seconds separating the riders on the road, although Phillis was twenty-three seconds adrift on corrected time. McIntyre was in fourth some eight seconds behind Phillis. Tragedy struck on the second lap when Tom Phillis crashed at Laurel Bank and sustained fatal injuries, this lap also claimed the life of A.J.S. mounted Kiwi Colin Meehan who crashed at Union Mills.

Bob McIntyre's race ended at Keppel Gate on the third lap with engine trouble Hailwood went on to beat rival Hocking by 5.6 seconds with Stastny nearly seven minutes behind in third. The death of close friend Tom Phillis had such an effect on Gary Hocking that he retired from motorcycle racing after winning Friday's Senior T.T.

Honda were eclipsed by Japanese rivals Suzuki in the two lap 50cc race when East German defector Ernst Degner won their first T.T., the Hondas of Luigi Tavari and Tommy Robb coming second and third respectively. The season ended with Honda claiming three World Championships through Taveri in the 125cc class and Redman in the 250cc and 350cc classes. The four cylinder machine proving its worth in the end although at tragic expense. The loss of Phillis was followed by the death of part-time Honda rider Bob McIntyre who was fatally injured at Oulton Park whilst riding his Norton.

The Redman Years

Honda withdrew from the 50cc Championship at the end of 1962 and concentrated on the 125, 250 and 350cc events. No new riders were brought into the team as they kept the previous years finishing line up. The indications from practice week on the Isle of Man suggested that Honda were not going to have things their own way in 1963. The four stroke four cylinder machines were finding life to be a lot tougher against the much improved two stroke air cooled disc-valve twin cylinder Yamahas.

Redman and Robb topped the leader board but were pushed hard by Fumio Ito and Tony Godfrey on their Yamahas. In the race Ito led after the first lap from Godfrey, Redman and Taveri with Takahashi fifth and Honda importer/motorcycle dealer Bill Smith in sixth. Godfrey suffered mechanical problems on the second lap and stopped at Kirk Michael to make adjustments. By the end of the lap Ito led Redman, Taveri, Takahashi and Smith; Godfrey pulled into the pits to make adjustments and then continued. Taveri and Takahashi both retired on the third lap and Tony Godfrey crashed heavily at Milntown suffering serious injury. Godfrey gained the dubious honour of being the first rider to be air lifted by helicopter to hospital. Redman carried on regardless and won his first T.T. by 27.2 seconds from Ito with an impressive Bill Smith in third and Tommy Robb fifth.

The Junior T.T. looked equally difficult for Honda with John Hartle topping the leader board on the Scuderia Duke Gilera from Robb, Hailwood (M.V.) and Redman. Honda had redeveloped their Junior machine and produced a four stroke four cylinder 350cc machine with a six speed gearbox that produced 54 bhp at 12,500 rpm. The race had a delayed start due to mist over the Mountain but once it was underway it could not have gone better for Jim Redman who started at number one and lead from start to finish. Mike Hailwood chased hard but could not better the Honda and his challenge faded on the fourth lap when his M.V. expired at Sulby. Tommy Robb didn't enjoy the same luck as Redman, after pitting at the end of the first lap he retired at the Graham Memorial on the second with engine failure. Redman comfortably won by 6 minutes 50 seconds from Hartle with Franta Stastny third.

Redman created history by achieving the Lightweight 250cc

and Junior 350cc double. This was
the first time this feat had been
achieved over the Mountain Course.
Bill Lomas achieved the 250/350cc
double in 1955 but the Lightweight
had been held over the 10.79 mile
Clypse course.

The omens for victory in the
125cc race were not good with the
Honda riders of Taveri, Takahashi
and Robb only fourth, fifth and sixth

**110.62 mph – 1978
Mike Hailwood
(Ducati)
First 110 mph lap
F1 T.T.**

Tommy Robb aboard Bob McIntyre's 1961 Honda RC 161 250cc machine, leaving the Grandstand during the Honda Anniversary Parade in 1998.
Courtesy Albert Cooper, The Mirror

The 1961 Honda RC 161 250cc machine complete with Mike Hailwood helmet and silver replica.

Courtesy Mike Hammonds

quickest in practice, trailing the Suzuki's of Hugh Anderson, Frank Perris and Bertie Schneider. The practice form was repeated in the weather-affected race with the Suzukis out pacing the Hondas to take the top three positions. The race was won by Hugh Anderson who lead home Perris, from Ernst Degner with Taveri fourth and Schnieder fifth, followed by the Hondas of Redman, Robb, Takahashi, Bryans and Dickinson.

The season ended with Taveri and Redman finishing second and third in the 125cc World Championship but with Redman attaining glory by matching his T.T. successes as the double 250cc and 350cc World Champion. Taveri also came third in the 350cc class.

The portents for the future were not good for Honda with the increasing competitiveness of the two stroke Suzuki and Yamaha machines and so much development was required on their four stroke engines to maintain their edge. They re-entered the 50cc Championship again in 1964 with a new twin cylinder machine that had a 33mm x 29.2mm engine that could rev to 20,000 rpm giving 13 bhp. This combined with an eight speed gearbox, gave it a top speed in excess of 100 mph. The four cylinder 125cc engine was also modified to produce 25 bhp at 16,000 rpm from a bore and stroke of 35mm x 32mm. The eight speed gearbox gave it a top speed of 120mph. Honda hoped that these developments would maintain their advantage over the two stroke competition.

The team was to contest all World Championship classes from 50cc to 350cc and included new members, Ulsterman Ralph Bryans, Southern Rhodesian Bruce Beale

The 1962 Honda RC 162 250cc machine

Courtesy Albert Cooper, The Mirror

(Left)
Union Mills at speed, Derek Minter upsetting the 'works' Honda by winning the 1962 Lightweight T.T.

(Bottom left)
Kunimitsu Takahashi, at Quarter Bridge during the 1998 Honda Anniversary Parade, aboard a 1962 Honda RC 162 250cc machine similar to the bike on which he crashed heavily , at Union Mills, during the 1962 Lightweight T.T.

Courtesy Mike Hammonds

and Japanese rider Isamu Kaseya. These joined the established stars of Redman, Taveri and Taniguchi; Tommy Robb having moved to the Yamaha camp. Bryans and Taniguchi contested the 50cc T.T. as did Taveri but he rode a Kreidler and not a works Honda. Bryans finished second with Taniguchi sixth.

Luigi Taveri had destroyed the opposition in practice for the 125cc T.T. by beating Anderson's lap record by over three miles per hour and

115.22 mph – 1980
Classic
**Joey Dunlop
(Yamaha)
First 115 mph Lap**

made himself firm favourite for the race. Under five seconds covered the leading four riders at the end of the first lap with Redman leading the Suzuki of Perris from Taveri and Bryans, Bruce Beale was in tenth but Suzuki favourite Anderson was out with engine trouble. The second lap saw the demise of Perris's challenge when his Suzuki faulted over the Mountain and he toured back to the Pits to retire. Redman now led Taveri from Bryans, with Beale up to ninth. Taveri certainly hadn't settled for second place and a combination of hard riding on his part, and poor information to Redman from his signalling stations, gave the likeable

Swiss victory by just 3 seconds. Taveri set lap and race records and Ralph Bryans completed the Honda domination by finishing third with Beale sixth.

Jim Redman was favourite for the Lightweight 250cc T.T. but was under threat from Yamaha mounted Phil Read and the M.Z. of Alan Shepherd. Shepherd was only given dispensation to ride on the Thursday of practice week after he had been passed fit by doctors, following injuries sustained from a crash on the continent. Excellent weather conditions prevailed as Redman lead the sixty-five strong field away in what was to be a war of attrition.

Redman led Read, from Shepherd and Taveri at the end of lap one, Beale was back in eleventh and Kaseya had crashed at Ballaugh Bridge and retired. Redman maintained his lead until the fourth lap where Read nosed in front only to retire before the end of the lap. This left Redman clear to win from Alan Shepherd with the distant Alberto Pagani on the Paton third, over 18 minutes behind. Taveri had retired on the fourth lap whilst in fifth position and Beale, on the fifth lap, whilst in seventh place. There were only eight finishers out of the sixty-five who started the race and remarkably seven different makes of

W

Jack Wood.

Jack Wood's forty year plus involvement in motorcycle sport culminated in becoming Clerk of the Course for the 1984 T.T. meeting. In his day he was a thoroughbred road racer winning the 1955 North West 200 Junior Race and racing successfully at the T.T. and MGP. Subsequently he has been Pit Marshal, Travelling Marshal, Scrutineer, Official Car Driver, Assistant Controller, Deputy Clerk of the Course for the MGP and then Clerk of the Course for that event in 1974. The role of Clerk of the Course is certainly high pressure - agreeing road closure

Jack Wood in the 1951 Senior Clubman's T.T.
Courtesy FoTTofinders Archive Research System

orders, drawing up racing and practice schedules, instructing marshals, arranging the distribution of fire extinguishers, radios etc., rider welfare, safety measures, reporting to the International Jury and, of course, deciding if the weather is suitable for racing.

machine! Honda, M.Z., Paton, C.Z., Yamaha, Aermacchi, Yamaha and Greeves.

Mike Hailwood was a non-starter for the Junior T.T., having influenza; the absence of the M.V. rider gave the Honda mounted Jim Redman a great chance of repeating his 250cc/350cc. race double of the previous year. Redman was not the sort who would look a gift horse in the mouth and a trouble free ride gave him a comfortable victory of over seven minutes from the A.J.S's of Phil Read and Mike Duff.

The season ended with Honda gaining second place in the 50cc World Championship with Ralph Bryans, first and second in the 125cc Championship with Taveri

and Redman, second in the 250cc Championship with Redman and finally first and second in the 350cc Championship with Redman and Beale.

The Two Stroke Challenge

The competition was getting tougher as each year went by and Honda were looking for even more power from their machines. This lead to the development of a six cylinder 250cc engine that had an eight speed gearbox and was capable of doing 150 mph and produced 53 bhp at 16,500 rpm. Alan Shepherd had signed for Honda at the end of the previous season and rode for them at the Japanese Grand Prix in

November 1964. Unfortunately for Alan, he crashed heavily and received serious head injuries. Following a test at Oulton Park he went to Amsterdam in May 1965 to discuss his future with Hisakazu Sekiguchi who was head of Honda Racing. It was decided at this meeting that Alan should be released from his contract, due to the effects of his injuries, and he prematurely retired from racing.

Ralph Bryans was the talk of practice week at the T.T. when he set a new but unofficial lap record in the 50cc class by beating Hugh Anderson's existing record by 37 seconds. The little Honda could not live up to its favourite tag in the race with Bryans retiring on the second lap; victory, however, went to team mate Luigi Taveri.

The 125cc race, held in perfect weather conditions, pitted the Honda's of Taveri, Bryans and Beale

Jim Redman's 1963 Honda RC 172 Four Cylinder 350cc machine that had a bore and stroke of 49 mm. x 45 mm.

113.58 mph – 1981 Graeme Crosby (Classic Suzuki) First 6 Lap race completed in under 2 hours.

against the new water cooled twin cylinder Yamaha's of Phil Read, Mike Duff and Yoshimi Katayama. At the end of the first lap only twelve seconds separated the first five riders, with the leaders Read, Duff and Katayama inside Taveri's lap record. Taveri had been experiencing front brake problems and was 5.8 seconds behind Katayama in fourth place but only

The start of the 1964 Ultra-Lightweight T.T., Ralph Bryans (5) push starts his four cylinder Honda alongside Frank Perris (6) with his twin cylinder Suzuki.

0.6 of a second ahead of Degner; Bruce Beale was out of the race having crashed and injured his hand. Race leader Read caught Taveri on the road on the second lap and the Honda was able to stay in the Yamaha's slip stream gaining valuable time, Katayama received a puncture at Creg-ny-Baa and retired. Read created history by becoming the first 125cc rider to lap at over 95 mph however this lap record was short lived because the hard charging Hugh Anderson lapped at 96.02 mph on his Suzuki. Taveri chased Read over the last lap but started to lose ground as they climbed the Mountain leaving him to fight Duff for second place. Read appeared to have the race in his

pocket until he approached Creg-ny-Baa and his Yamaha spluttered and went on to one cylinder! It wasn't long before Taveri screamed past Read and he now had to gain at least twenty seconds in the last couple of miles to take the winner's laurels. Taveri crossed the line first, the seconds ticked by, but Read came into view and limped across the line to secure Yamaha's first T.T. victory by just 5.8 seconds. Duff's Yamaha had experienced the same problem as Read thus giving Taveri second place by 15.2 seconds. Ralph Bryans brought his Honda home in sixth place. There was delight in the Honda camp because this was the first time this season that they had finished a 125cc race!

The 250cc Lightweight race again pitted Honda against Yamaha with Redman and Beale up against Read, Duff and Bill Ivy. Redman lead the field away at number one but was greatly concerned about Phil Read who started twenty seconds later at number five. Read was determined to catch Redman and by the end of the first lap he nearly had him in his sights, being only four seconds behind on the road. This opening lap of Read's was nothing short of sensational! It was the first time the 100 mph barrier had been broken by a 250cc

100.31 mph – 1981
Barrie Smith
(Yamaha)
Fastest Lap
F 3 T.T.

machine, and this from a standing start! Read's lap time was 22 minutes 38.2 seconds a speed of 100.01 mph. All Read needed to do was sit behind Redman for the next five laps and the race would be his, however the temptation to show his dominance was too great!! Read overtook Redman going up the Mountain Mile and started to forge ahead. Read's delight of passing Redman was short lived because the Yamaha seized before he had reached the East Mountain Box and he was out. Redman maintained his pace and took 1.2 seconds off Read's lap record to set a new mark of 100.09 mph. The race was now in Redman's control and he went on to record his third consecutive 250cc T.T. victory by 3 minutes 40.6 seconds from Mike Duff with Frank Perris's Suzuki third, Provini's Benelli fourth, Stastny's Jawa fifth, Dave William's Mondial sixth and Giberto Milani's Aermacchi seventh. Seven different makes of machine in the top seven places of the twenty-five finishers out of seventy-six starters. Bruce Beale retired his Honda on the last lap whilst holding fifth place.

The Junior T.T. gave Redman the opportunity of winning the 250cc/350cc double for the third

year running. This year the competition was intense with the Honda's of Redman and Beale up against Phil Read's Yamaha, Mike Hailwood and Italian newcomer Giacomo Agostini on the M.V.

Agustas and Derek Woodman on the M.Z. Honda were determined to create history and put all their efforts into helping Redman achieve his goal. The M.V. three of Hailwood and Agostini had been specially

Team mates in 1966, Ralph Bryans and Sturat Graham chat about old times during the Honda Anniversary celebrations in 1998.

Courtesy Mike Hammonds

adapted with larger petrol tanks and changed gearing to cope with the pace and thirst of the machines. Honda had timed the gravity petrol fillers so that they knew exactly how long it would take to fill the tank. At Redman's pit stop one mechanic would operate the filler whilst the other would time him with a stop watch, stopping him after exactly nineteen seconds!!

A blistering first lap saw only 54 seconds separating the top five with Hailwood setting a new lap record of 102.85 mph in 22 minutes 0.6 seconds. He lead Redman by 20.4 seconds from Read, Agostini and Woodman. As Hailwood passed the Pits he waved an oil-covered boot, much to the concern of the M.V. mechanics; however it didn't appear to hamper him because he equalled

his lap record on the second lap to maintain his lead. Woodman had relegated Agostini to fifth but by the end of the third lap Agostini had regained his position behind Hailwood, Redman and Read. Bruce Beale was making good progress in sixth place, with Hailwood and Redman averaging over 100 mph.

The leading pair came into the Pits at virtually the same time at the end of the third lap. Hailwood was leading the race by 27.6 seconds but had started 30 seconds behind Redman in the race. Predictably, Redman's pit stop was slick and he got away first, the crowd on the Grandstand were willing Hailwood to rejoin the affray but he appeared to have a problem. The mechanics worked furiously on the back wheel of the M.V. to take the slack out of the

loose drive chain as well as wiping away the oil from the rear tyre and forks. The tension in the crowd was increasing as Agostini came into his pit adjacent to Hailwood's, but the cheers rang out as Hailwood eventually got away after a stoppage of 2 minutes 45 seconds. Redman was now comfortably leading the race with Read in second place, over a minute behind. The endeavours of the M.V. mechanics were in vain as Hailwood retired at Sarah's Cottage with a stretched drive chain much to the disappointment of the thousands of fans around the course.

Victory was now well within Redman's grasp and he didn't let it slip, creating history by becoming the first rider to win three consecutive Junior T.T.s. He led home Phil Read by 1 minute 52.2 seconds with

The famous 1965 Six cylinder Honda RC 164 250cc machine that had a bore and stroke of 39mm. x 34.5mm. This gave an engine capacity of 247.3cc.

110.03 mph – 1983
Con Law
(EMC)
First 110 mph Lap
250cc machine

Agostini third and Beale in fourth. Redman's record breaking race time of 2 hours 14 minutes 52.2 seconds gave him a race average of 100.72 mph. This was the first time that the 100 mph race average had been broken in the Junior T.T. Jim Redman had immortalised his name in T.T. folklore by becoming the first rider to win the Lightweight and Junior T.T.s three years running and today he remains the only rider to have achieved this feat. The season ended with Honda winning the 50cc World Championship through Ralph Bryans with Taveri runner up. Redman won the 350cc World Championship but could only manage third place in the 250cc Championship behind Read and Duff.

Hailwood Returns

The plans for the 1966 season were well advanced and Honda had developed a 500cc four cylinder machine to contest the World Championship. This bike had a bore and stroke of 57mm x 48mm which could be revved up to 12,700rpm giving 90 bhp. Honda had promised team leader Jim Redman a chance of winning the "Blue Riband" 500cc World Championship but also wanted an experienced rider to support the team. To this end Honda secured the services of the current and four times 500cc World Champion, Mike Hailwood. Hailwood joined the team knowing that he would have to play second fiddle to Redman in the large class but would have first choice machines for the

250cc and 350cc Championships.

The National Seaman's Strike lead to the postponement of the Isle of Man T.T. from its traditional June date, it would now be held after the Manx Grand Prix in September. Jim Redman had crashed his 500cc Honda at the Belgium Grand Prix and injured himself sufficiently to put himself out for the season. Redman decided during his recuperation that enough was enough and he retired from World Championship racing. Redman's departure from the team left the way open for Hailwood to try and retain his crown although he had not scored a point after the first three races.

At the T.T. Honda contested every solo race with a team of Bryans, Taveri, Hailwood and Stuart Graham. The three lap 50cc race was won by Bryans with Taveri second. Honda machinery took nine of the first twelve bikes to finish.

Mist delayed the start of the 125cc T.T. in which the five cylinder Hondas were up against the very fast and competitive Yamaha twins. Hailwood and Bryans appeared to be well down on power as the race got under way, this was attributed to a change in the atmospheric conditions as the mist lifted and the sun shone causing carburation difficulties. The problem didn't seem to effect Taveri but he lost precious time when he overshot at Ballacraine. However none of this could take away the brilliant rides of the Yamaha pair of Read and Ivy. Ivy was second to Read at the end of the

first lap but went on to win in record breaking time by 33.4 seconds from Read with Hugh Anderson's Suzuki third, the Hondas of Hailwood, Bryans and Taveri could only manage sixth, seventh and eighth respectively.

The Honda "six" of Hailwood and Graham were up against the Yamaha "fours" of Read and Ivy in the Lightweight 250cc race. Hailwood started the race forty seconds behind arch rival Read and was determined to catch the Yamaha man on the road. Hailwood had Read well within his sights at Creg-ny-Baa and he crossed the start and finish line in

X

Excelsior.

With the exception of 1926 Excelsior machines were seen largely in the Lightweight class at every T.T. meeting from 1923 to 1955. Two victories were achieved, both Lightweights and both by men called Syd - Crabtree in 1929 and Gleaves in 1933. The last man to complete the full race distance on an Excelsior was J.J.I. Sparrow, finishing 16th in the 250cc of 1954.

(Left)
Ralph Bryans, at the Gooseneck, on his way to third place in the 1967 Lightweight T.T.

(Below left)
An array of 1960's Honda machinery seen during the Fiftieth Anniversary of the Honda Motor Corporation on the Isle of Man.
No. 10 is a 1965 Honda RC 115 50cc twin, No. 11 a 1966 Honda RC 145 125cc, No. 9 a 1961 Honda RC 161 250cc, Nos. 8 & 2 are 1962 Honda RC 162 250cc.

Courtesy Mike Hammonds

the Yamaha's slip stream. Hailwood had shattered the lap record and now had the Yamaha trailing in his wake. The pace was too hot for Read and the Yamaha to cope with and he retired at Ginger Hall on the second lap. Hailwood was now in a class of his own and he went on to win by nearly six minutes from team mate Graham. Hailwood's new lap and race records bettered the

97.21 mph – 1984
Senior
Dave Roper
(Matchless)
Fastest Lap
Historic T.T.

existing Junior T.T. records and was the first time the 100 mph race barrier had been broken by a 250cc machine

The Junior Race brought the much awaited clash between the Honda mounted Hailwood and his former team mate Giacomo Agostini on the M.V. Unfortunately the battle of the gladiators didn't last too long with Hailwood retiring at Bishops Court with a broken exhaust valve on the first lap. Agostini went on to record his first T.T. win from Peter Williams on an A.J.S.

The Senior T.T. again pitted Hailwood against Agostini but this time the battle would last the full distance. To stand any chance of retaining his World Championship Hailwood had to win this race with only the Italian Grand Prix to come. Hailwood started the race twenty seconds in front of his rival and was determined not to let the Italian catch him or see him on the road. The Honda man got off to a flyer and lead Agostini by six seconds after the first lap with a lap of 105.82 mph. The pace soared and Hailwood set a new course outright lap record on the second circuit with a speed of 107.07 mph, but he hadn't shaken "Ago" off his tail because he lapped at 106.68 m.ph. The weather closed in on the fourth lap and rain started to fall on the west side of the Island, this, combined with front brake problems, eased the Italian's pace leaving Hailwood unchallenged for victory. His victory margin was 2 minutes 37.8 seconds over Agostini who in turn led third placed man

Chris Conn on the Norton by over eight minutes.

Hailwood may have won the battle but Agostini won the war by winning the Italian Grand Prix and winning the World Championship, Hailwood's hopes faded when he retired with gearbox trouble having to settle for the runner-up spot. Hailwood did however win both the 250cc and 350cc World Championships, Taveri won the 125cc title and was third in the 50cc class and Bryans managed to come runner up in 50cc and third in the 125cc Championships.

The End of an Era

The Honda "raison d'etre" for racing was to sell their production bikes to the European mass market. This was now in decline and the emphasis had shifted to the United States and thus the motivation to go racing had greatly diminished. Honda decided to stop development of their racing machines at the end of the 1966 season and withdrew from the 50cc and 125cc classes altogether. They agreed to let Hailwood and Bryans ride existing machines in the larger World Championship classes during 1967.

The sixtieth anniversary of the T.T. Races was celebrated on their traditional dates after the previous years impromptu change. Hailwood and Bryans entered their partially factory supported Hondas. In the Lightweight 250cc T.T. their main challenge would once again come from the Yamaha mounted Phil Read

and Bill Ivy. Just 2.5 seconds separated the first three after the opening lap with Hailwood marginally in front of Read and Ivy; by the end of the second lap Hailwood had increased his lead to 13 seconds over Read and 22 seconds over Ivy. Hailwood's lap time of 21 minutes 39.8 seconds was a new lap record of 105.5 mph. Ivy retired on the fourth lap promoting Bryans into third place and the top three remained unchanged until the finish. Hailwood had won his tenth T.T. equalling the record of Stanley Woods, setting new lap and race records. Fittingly one of the first people to congratulate Hailwood was Stanley Woods who was more than generous with his appreciation of his record equalling feat.

The Diamond Jubilee Junior T.T. brought another head to head encounter between Hailwood and Agostini with Renzo Pasolini on the Benelli, Derek Woodman and Heinz Rosner on the M.Z.s giving added interest. The Honda rider had not only topped the practice leader board but had unofficially broken the lap record as well to make him firm favourite. The opening lap was nothing short of astonishing with Hailwood setting a new course absolute record of 107.73 mph., leaving Agostini struggling 49 seconds behind followed by Pasolini and Rosner. The lead increased to 63 seconds at the end of the second lap and to over two minutes by the end of the third with the leader board remaining unchanged. Hailwood pressed on regardless, but Pasolini and Rosner both retired on

Y

Yamaha.

The most successful marque in terms of T.T. victories is Yamaha. Phil Read was the company's first victor - the 1965 Ultra-Lightweight; the first placing was secured by Fumio Itoh in the 1961 250cc race when he finished 6th. . . . but who was the first entry? That honour fell to Californian Sonny Angel in 1960 riding a 5 speed 250 twin. Unfortunately, the American failed to qualify, his machine continually suffering from burned and seized pistons. Though the ACU offered to waive qualification, Angel did not start.

One of the early Yamaha competitors - Japan's Tansharu Noguchi aboard his 125cc machine at Governor's Bridge in 1961. *Courtesy FoTTofinders Archive Research System*

the fourth lap elevating Derek Woodman to third by the end of the race. For the second race running Hailwood had set new lap and race records and this gave him great heart for the Senior race to come.

Arguably one of the greatest, if not "The Greatest" race in the history of the T.T. Races was the Diamond Jubilee Senior T.T. Held on Friday 16th June 1967 it was a battle royal between the ill-handling Honda "four" of Hailwood and the deep throated three cylinder M.V. of Agostini. Hailwood was first away at number four and Agostini followed, thirty seconds later, at number nine in hot pursuit. The radio commentary points

reported that the Italian was leading and gaining rapidly on the Honda man at each point around the course. Hailwood gave the "thumbs down" signal as he flashed past the Grandstand to start his second lap, even though he had broken the existing lap record with a speed of 107.37 mph. This new lap record didn't stand for very long because Agostini crossed the line within 18 seconds of Hailwood to become the first man to lap the course in under 21 minutes with a speed of 108.30 mph. Hailwood had got the message that he was losing ground and he took the "bucking steer" of a Honda to its limits and reduced the deficit by four seconds at the end of

the second lap, setting a new absolute lap record of 108.77 mph. This record would last eight years. The pit stops loomed at the end of the third lap and Hailwood was first in to refuel. This was not to be an

113.41 mph – 1988 Steve Hislop (Yamaha) Fastest Lap F II T.T.

ordinary refuelling stop as the twist grip on the Honda had come loose and a hammer was required to knock it back into place. Agostini arrived at the Grandstand amongst all the confusion holding a two second lead and stopping in his pit just a couple in front of Hailwood. Hailwood was first away but his lengthy stop had cost him 47.8 seconds whereas "Ago" was out in 37.8 seconds giving him a twelve second lead. This differential was maintained throughout the lap but remarkably by the time Agostini got to Kirk Michael on the fifth lap the lead had been reduced to just three seconds. At Ramsey, Hailwood was leading by one second but they were level on corrected time at the Les Graham Memorial on the Mountain. Hailwood streaked

through the Grandstand to start this last lap unaware that he had an unassailable lead!! Agostini's chain had broken at Windy Corner, putting him out of the running. He free wheeled back to the pits but by-passed Governors Dip enforcing his retirement. It was an emotional and bitterly disappointed Italian in the paddock as Hailwood crossed the line to take his 12th T.T. victory out of 32 starts. Hailwood had received a signal at Ballacraine to say Agostini was out but still completed the race in record breaking time of 2 hours 08 minutes 36.2 seconds an average speed of 105.62 mph.

In the World Championship history repeated itself with Agostini again winning the last Grand Prix at Monza with Hailwood retiring. This

left them on equal points with five victories each but "Ago" took the title by virtue of his three second places compared with Hailwood's two. Hailwood won both the 250cc and 350cc World championships with Bryans third in the 350cc

Honda withdrew completely from road racing at the end of 1967 and Hailwood, like Surtees before him, moved into car racing. Honda had left their mark indelibly on the racing world and the T.T. in particular. They contested 27 races at the T.T. winning 18 and entered 25 World Championships winning 16. This was an end of an era but only the end of a chapter in the history of the T.T. Honda and Hailwood would return to the Island in the future and gain further success but, alas, not as a team.

Z

Walter Zeller.

Last in the alphabetical index of T.T. riders is the wealthy Bavarian Walter Zeller who raced with great success for the BMW concern. Entering the meeting in just three races - the Seniors of '53, '56 and '57, he had two retirements and a creditable 4th position in 1956. The only rider of a solo BMW in the Island that year he was never out of the top 6, eventually finishing behind John Surtees, John Hartle and Jack Brett.

Last in the alphabet, but not last in the race, German, Walter Zeller in action.

ON APPEAL – BLACK FRIDAY

The Honda works team of Ron Haslam, Joey Dunlop and Alex George rode in traditional black leathers and on machines with black fairings in the 1981 1000cc Classic Race. This was by way of protest against events that occurred earlier in the week:

Suzuki works rider, New Zealander Graeme Crosby, had been allocated start number 16 in the previous Saturday's Formula One Race, but wasn't on the start line because his machine was having a rear slick tyre fitted. He started, therefore, at the rear of the field, but it was announced that he would not be given a time allowance.

At the end of the first lap Dunlop led Mick Grant (Suzuki) by 7 seconds, but Grant narrowed the gap to within 3 seconds on the next circuit. The Suzuki rider's race ended at Ballacraine on the next lap and so, at half distance, the order was Dunlop, Haslam (70 seconds in arrears), Sam McClements, John Newbold, Kevin Wrettom and Alex George, with Crosby circulating in

12th place. Haslam was in and out of the pits quickly at the end of lap 4, but Dunlop had a longer stay when he changed a wheel. Haslam led by 52 seconds at the end of lap 5.

Crosby really stepped on the gas during the final lap (6), breaking the lap record at 113.70mph, circulating in 19 minutes 54.6 seconds, finishing third behind the two works Hondas. Ron Haslam was declared the winner but it was announced that Suzuki had lodged a protest well before the race was over against the decision that Crosby should not be allowed time for starting at the rear of the field.

The protest was upheld by the International Jury and his time was re-assessed, and despite a counter-protest, Crosby was declared the winner - Honda were not happy!

To complete a miserable week for Honda, Graeme Crosby completed the double when he won the Classic in 1 hour 59 minutes 34.8 seconds; the first time a six lap race had been completed in under two hours. Dunlop did put up the fastest lap (115.40mph) but retired on lap five, joining Haslam, who had gone out two laps earlier. Mick Grant finished 30 seconds behind Crosby, with George in third.

**121.00 mph – 1991
Steve Hislop
(FI Honda)
First
120 mph Average
6 Lap race**

STRANGE BUT TRUE

The race programme of the '90s is dominated by Yamaha, Honda, Suzuki and Ducati, but what of the past? Many a strange machine has leapt Ballaugh Bridge, scratched around Ramsey Hairpin and climbed the Mountain . . . perhaps the most famous was the **Shuttleworth Snap** on which George Formby practised, but didn't race . . . He actually pushed over the line to win with the colourful works **Rainbow**!

Back in the real world, few will remember the versatile **Matador** charging around to a handful of leaderboard positions, notably third in the 1924 Sidecar in the capable hands of A. Tinkler. What about the **Trump**, which didn't pull any aces in 1910, or the **Royal Ruby**, which wasn't crowned in glory a few years later? No help was required for the **SOS** to finish 10th in the '29 Lightweight, but divine intervention couldn't help A.E. Dawson's **Pope Special** in the '63 50cc race.

The **Diamond** competed regularly in the '20s and early '30s, but failed to sparkle; the **Peerless** stood on its own as it retired from the 1913 Senior; not enough spice was available for the **Cayenne** to finish the same race. The **Centaur** wasn't man enough in 1910, the **Coventry Mascot** needed all the help it could get as it retired from the '23 Junior and the **Chase** failed to make the running in the last race before the Great War. Not enough magic was available for the **Merlin** to complete the three laps of the '66 Ultra-Lightweight, but the **Monk Special** did receive help from somewhere two years earlier in coming home 35th in the Junior. Chains couldn't keep the **Pankhurst Special** down in its only race - 10th in the '51 125cc; the **Sun** shone quite consistently with five top twenty finishes out of six starts and R. H. Bacon's **Bits** did manage to cross the finish line in 25th and last place in the first ever 50cc race.

FORTY-SEVEN MACHINES

A complete list of the 47 different makes of machine that have been victorious in T.T. races. Also included are the rider, race and year involved in the machine's first, and perhaps only, victory.

1. **Matchless**
    Charlie Collier
    Single Cylinder
    1907

2. **Norton**
    Rem Fowler
    Twin Cylinder
    1907

3. **Triumph**
    Jack Marshall
    Single Cylinder
    1908

4. **D.O.T.**
    Harry Reed
    Twin Cylinder
    1908

5. **Indian**
    Oliver Godfrey
    Senior
    1911

6. **Humber**
    Percy Evans
    Junior
    1911

7. **Scott**
    Frank Appleby
    Senior
    1912

8. **Douglas**
    Harry Bashall
    Junior
    1912

9. **N.U.T.**
    Hugh Mason
    Junior
    1913

10. **Rudge**
    Cyril Pullin
    Senior
    1914

11. **AJS**
    Eric Williams
    Junior
    1914

12. **Sunbeam**
    Tommy de la Hay
    Senior
    1920

123.61 mph – 1992
Carl Fogarty
(Senior Yamaha)
Outright
Lap Record
Smashed

13. **Levis**
R.O. Clark
Lightweight
1920

14. **New Imperial**
Doug Prentice
Lightweight
1921

15. **New Gerrard**
Jack Porter
Lightweight
1923

16. **Cotton**
Stanley Woods
Junior
1923

17. **HRD**
Howard Davies
Senior
1925

18. **Rex Acme**
Wal Handley
Junior
1925

19. **Velocette**
Alec Bennett
Junior
1926

20. **OK Supreme**
Frank Longman
Lightweight
1928

21. **Excelsior**
Sid Crabtree
Lightweight
1929

22. **Moto Guzzi**
Stanley Woods
Lightweight
1935

23. **DKW**
Ewald Kluge
Lightweight
1938

24. **BMW**
Georg Meier
Senior
1939

25. **Benelli**
Ted Mellors
Lightweight
1939

26. **Vincent HRD**
J.D. Daniels
Senior Clubmans
1948

27. **BSA**
H. Clark
Junior Clubmans
1949

28. **Mondial**
Cromie McCandless
Ultra Lightweight
1951

29. **MV Agusta**
Cecil Sandford
Ultra Lightweight
1952

30. **NSU**
Rupert Hollaus
Ultra Lightweight
1954

31. **Gilera**
Geoff Duke
Senior
1955

32. **Honda**
Mike Hailwood
Ultra Lightweight
1961

33. **Suzuki**
Ernst Degner
50cc
1962

94

34. **Yamaha**
Phil Read
Ultra Lightweight
1965

35. **Bultaco**
Bill Smith
250cc Production
1967

36. **Derbi**
Barrie Smith
50cc
1968

37. **Dunstall Dominator**
Ray Pickerell
750cc Production
1968

38. **Ossa**
Trevor Burgess
250cc Production
1968

39. **Ducati**
Tony Rodgers
250cc Production
1969

40. **Kawasaki**
Dave Simmonds
Ultra Lightweight
1969

41. **Yamsel**
Tony Jefferies
Junior
1971

42. **Konig**
Rolf Steinhausen
Sidecar (500)
1975

43. **Armstrong CCM**
Steve Tonkin
Junior (250)
1981

44. **Waddon-Erlich**
Con Law
Junior (250)
1982

45. **EMC**
Con Law
Junior (250)
1983

46. **Aermacchi**
Steve Cull
350cc Historic T.T.
1984

47. **Barton Phoenix**
Nigel Rollason
Sidecar (B)
1986

Derbyshire, Windle, Sabre, DMR and NRTH Ireson makes have been victorious in the Sidecar class during recent years. Their names, however, are based on frames not engines.

120.70 mph – 1998
Jim Moodie
(Honda)
First 120mph Lap
Production T.T.

Closing Thoughts . . .

Scenes from the 1907 T.T. Races - courtesy FoTTofinders Archive Research System.

Left, not right, and foot hard down at Kirk Michael corner.

At speed through the houses of Peel.